Faith is not Important... it is *Everything!*

Common sense reasons for nonbelievers
to reconsider Christianity

Mike Gilles

Inscript

Bladensburg, MD

Faith
is not
Important...
it is
Everything!

Published by
Inscript Books
A division of Dove Christian Publishers
P.O. Box 611
Bladensburg, MD 20710-0611
www.dovechristianpublishers.com

To my wife, Marion,
whose positive initial review of an early draft
encouraged me to make this
book a reality. Thank you, Dear!

Table of Contents

PREFACE
Why This Book?

There certainly doesn't seem to be a shortage of books on faith or Jesus Christ and Christianity, so does the world need another? I'd like to think the answer is yes. Many books on the topic go deep into philosophy and theology to support a faith in Christianity, a belief in the divinity of Jesus Christ. In this book, I intend to present a case for Christianity in the most basic terms possible. I hope that by using only basic reasoning, logic, and good old common sense, you might become convinced of the very thing millions of Christians around the world already believe—that Jesus is indeed the Son of God, and the only path to heaven is by faith in Him.

I know some have been wounded or just plain turned off to the very concept of 'religion' for a multitude of different reasons. Maybe a priest or pastor has offended you, or maybe it was someone who claimed to be 'religious' and quite possibly even a 'Christian' whom you saw as a horrible example of how someone making those claims should look and act. I'm asking you to put all of that aside, as well as all of your preconceived feelings about God and religion, just long enough to read as I present my case. I have no intention of using any razzle-dazzle in an attempt to turn you into a believer. However, I intend to present what I believe to be compelling evidence to explain why so many have already found their way to Christ.

Christianity is not about your hurt feelings or your past bad experiences, and it is not about the people who may have caused you to feel the way you do about the topic, because this isn't about them; it's about you and a potential relationship with your Creator.

I also know there are those (including some of you reading this right now) who don't want anything to do with churches because they are full of hypocrites and, heaven forbid, even sinners. There are hypocrites everywhere; always has been and always will be, but finding them is not my job or yours. However, when it comes to sinners, I take joy in the fact that churches may very well be filled with sinners. Jesus established the church as a hospital for sinners. Those that are well do not need a hospital, and if the churches are drawing sinners and hypocrites in, I say "amen"; they are fulfilling their purpose. If there were no sinners and hypocrites, there would have been no need for Jesus. But we are all sinners, maybe not all hypocrites, but regardless, we all need saving just the same.

If you are not currently a 'believer,' or if you are just 'kind of a believer' and maybe aren't quite sure what that means, yet you were curious enough to pick up this book and read this far, please continue to read. Don't stop now. Please read on because you are the very person this book was written for.

Some years ago, I had the opportunity to preach regularly for a few years in a small semi-rural church my wife and I had a part in establishing in Michigan's Upper Peninsula. I closed every message with an opportunity for anyone who had not yet accepted Jesus Christ as their personal Lord and Savior to do so right then by simply and privately saying this prayer: "Lord Jesus, forgive me for my sins. I do believe you are the Son of God and you died to save me from the consequences of my sins. I ask you to enter my heart and help me to change my life." One day, I received an email complaint from a member of the congregation saying I was making salvation sound too easy. I had to tell him, and I am telling you now, it is *just that easy*. There is nothing magical about the specific words of the prayer, so it doesn't have to be those exact words. You merely need to acknowledge Jesus Christ as God, Lord, and Savior and ask forgiveness and help in changing your life.

God chose to create man with the ability to screw up and the ability to make decisions, good and bad. He never intended for us to be perfect; He certainly hoped we would be, but clearly, He also knew giving us a free will may just have been the kiss of death when it comes to perfection. It would not be reasonable for God or anyone else to think that creating us with the ability to make free choices would not result in us messing up at least occasionally.

God is no different from any loving parent who knows their beautiful child will one day grow into an adult, and like any good parent, they want nothing but the best for their child. They also know that at some point, they no longer have any control over that child, and that child may make a lot of bad choices in life. But God, unlike that parent, could have created His children without the ability to choose, without the option of not following His wishes and without any choice but to love Him. He chose to go a different route because He wanted His children to love Him because they wanted to, not because they had to. Love has to be a choice, freely given.

In the case of mankind, it didn't take long for the first screw-up to occur. The Bible tells us that when God created the first man and woman, He placed them in the Garden of Paradise and told them the entire garden was theirs, and they could enjoy everything in it, with one single exception. The Bible tells us it was the fruit of one tree in the middle of the garden. With all the fruit of all the other trees, they just weren't enough. Man just couldn't resist and chose to break the one and only rule God had given them. One rule! That choice meant the end of life in the perfect garden, and unfortunately, it meant mankind would forever pay the price. Man had opened Pandora's Box, discovered sin, and it seems we haven't stopped sinning since.

Very briefly, a little about me, and very little because I don't want this book in any way to be about me. I only want to share what I know about God. Most 'born again' Christians I know (and I'll get to a definition of 'born again' a little further in the book) can recite the exact date the light went on and they accepted Jesus Christ as their Lord and Savior. Many know exactly where they were and remember the exact circumstances. I can't. I didn't experience a single 'ah-ha' moment at any point in my life. I didn't come to Christ at a particular time or at a particular event. I was born into a Christian family, went to Catholic schools and spent my high school years in a seminary studying to be a priest. Yet, I never really knew Jesus nor had any kind of relationship with Him. I had lost my way throughout a major portion of my life, during which Jesus was not on my radar.

However, I did come to know Jesus over a long period, and I do know that sometime after 1996, the process began in earnest. I'm sure the seeds were planted sometime before that, going back to my Catholic upbringing. What I do know is when my wife and I were married, we made a decision to change our lives and make Jesus Christ a central and integral part of our life and our marriage, and today I am a born again Christian, and Jesus Christ is the Lord of my life.

When I think about specific dates, I am reminded about a humorous scene from the movie "Miss Congeniality." Now, this has absolutely nothing to do with accepting Christ, just an amusing story about dates. The movie centers around a beauty pageant, and in this scene, the pageant host is questioning the contestants, and he asks, "please describe for me the perfect date." The young contestant thinks for a moment and then says, "April 25th, because it is warm but not too warm and you may only need a light jacket." Obviously, not the answer the judge was looking for. But the point being, dates are not important; when and how you may come to know Jesus is not important; just doing it is!

The last thing Jesus ever intended was that His teachings would ever be considered complicated, or the Bible would need someone to interpret it for us. It is extremely unfortunate that for more than 2,000 years, some churches have done exactly that—made an uncomplicated teaching complicated.

Since you have actually selected this book and read this far, I pray you will continue and allow your mind to be opened to the possibility that your lack of faith is merely because you have never been exposed to the truth in a way that actually makes sense.

There is no mystique to Christianity. Jesus never intended anything other than to keep it simple and to make salvation freely available to everyone, and I do mean everyone. He died to save all of us, not a select few.

Mike Gilles

CHAPTER 1

Is There a God?

Since this book is about Christianity and shows that Jesus Christ existed and not only just existed, but that He is the Son of God, it seems appropriate that we would first have to deal with the existence of God before we can deal with His Son.

I know I cannot assume everyone reading this book is an atheist, but if you call yourself an atheist or are not sure what you believe, this chapter is for you. I will, however, assume that maybe you do believe in God or at least a god of some kind, someone above our 'pay grade,' someone who at the very least sort of controls things. There seem to be several levels of belief; there are those convinced there is no god; those who believe there probably is some sort of a god, and those who do not doubt God but may not be sure about Jesus.

To start with, I'm going to ask you once again to keep an open mind as we travel through this book and to forget any of your preconceived ideas or things you may have heard or believed in the past. I'm asking you to let a clear head, logic, and common sense take the place of those preconceptions. This is not a mind game or a trick; I just want you to take a good look at the evidence and think for yourself when it comes to drawing any conclusions.

Think about this: if Christopher Columbus believed all he had been taught, he certainly would never have set sail to the west to find a route to the far east, since the accepted belief at the time was the world was flat and if one traveled too far to the west or any direction, for that matter, they would fall off the end of the earth into the abyss.

We could never have traveled to the moon or sent unmanned probes to other planets if we had continued to believe the science that existed up and through the middle ages: that all the planets revolved around the earth. The early church excommunicated, kicked out, those who taught such heresy, that the sun, not the earth, was the center of the universe.

Over time, man has disproved so many things we once believed to be facts. If scientific research continued to assume there just are things that cannot be accomplished, new discoveries most certainly would be few and far between. Thankfully, we are no longer guided by the concept that it can't be done. We would never have tried to find cures for cancer, and we would not be routinely transplanting organs, because I am sure at some point in our history, we just 'knew' this was not possible. I am asking you to proceed with the same kind of open-mindedness and allow yourself to accept that what you may have heard or believed about God and Jesus Christ just may not be true. You are going to read, in this and the following chapters, things that may go against what you may currently believe, but I ask you to decide on your own what is and is not truth. The earth is not flat!

In today's world, probably more than at any time in our history, it seems like we want to deny the existence of God. It's as though we have gotten 'too big for our britches'; this is somewhat of an outdated term maybe, but it seems to apply here. In the 21st century, we have become so 'enlightened' and so arrogant, we think we no longer need God. We tend to look to ourselves as the 'end-all.'

A Wall Street Journal/NBC News survey conducted between August 10-14, 2019, found that millennials no longer view patriotism, faith or families as important as Americans once did.[1] So, what does this mean? What is important to millennials? It seems to indicate that millennials have become more self-absorbed than in past generations. It appears that they are becoming a generation that puts self at the center of their universe. The survey shows a 9% drop in patriotism, a 12% drop in faith and 9% in having families. These changes have all happened in just the past 21 years; if this trend continues, and there is no reason to assume it will not, what will the priorities be 21 years from now? What will the society of the future look like if future generations continue to become more concerned with self than God, family or country?

Getting back to the God topic, a theory among some atheists is that belief in a god may have been something primitive man used to explain things they didn't understand. However, in this era of such 'intelligence,' we don't really need anything or anyone other than ourselves, certainly not a god. Can't science explain away any need for a god?

If you classify yourself as an atheist, you need to be honest with yourself and ask yourself the hard questions. Do you refuse to believe because you are angry at a God who can allow evil in the world and allow bad things to happen? I've certainly heard that one before. In this case, how can you be angry at someone who doesn't exist? Only you can honestly confirm why you choose not to believe. I am not going to tell you that you are wrong to feel the way you do. There is never any wrong feeling. You feel what you feel. I may not agree with the reasoning behind your feeling and I am merely asking your indulgence as you continue reading. Keep your mind open to possibilities.

In the preface, I asked you to rely on common sense and logic as well as your ability to examine facts, then use reasoning to draw conclusions. Look at the magnificence and complexity of the human being as well as everything around us and in the universe and beyond. Can all this just be the result of a big bang, evolution, or anything other than intelligent design?

Let's start with man; think about how intricate we are, how every part of us functions. What is truly unique is what we are capable of accomplishing. We have emotions, feelings; we feel love, and most importantly, we are capable of choice. We make these choices based on reasoning, our ability to think, analyze and draw conclusions. Some animals, at least to some degree, can experience some sort of feelings, but man alone is unique in the ability to appreciate and enjoy such things as art, music, and intimacy. Not only can man appreciate all these things, but we are also capable of creating the very things that we appreciate. Is this all just random chance, evolving from pond scum and developing into who we are? Not only can we enjoy and appreciate everything around us but we are capable of reason, capable of invention, capable of solving problems, and capable of creating beauty in the form of things like art and music. We don't just have feelings, but we think, we enjoy, we feel anger, sadness, happiness, and find joy in people and things around us.

Some animals have learned to use 'tools.' For example, some apes can pick up a stick, poke it into an anthill and draw out the stick full of ants to eat. Certainly, this is a basic use of a tool, and there is evidence of others in the animal kingdom using 'tools' to dig or perform other tasks. Can we assume that this is a part of their evolutionary process? Can we reasonably assume, maybe a billion years from now, an ape will be capable of reasoning and thinking similar to humans? If apes were doing these things thousands of years ago, why haven't they come any further in their evolutionary process in all this time? Why haven't we seen mankind continue to evolve over all of our known history? Our knowledge-base certainly has grown, but is there any evidence that we as a species have evolved?

If we evolved or grew out of single cells growing in a swamp, explain why humanity seems to have grown out of a single area, maybe even a particular swamp, then populated the globe. Wouldn't some form of evolution have happened, possibly occurring simultaneously, in all kinds of locations on the planet? Might we not then expect to see a variety of advanced beings inhabiting the planet? If single cells combined and started the process in, for the sake of argument, a swamp, wouldn't it be logical to assume that cells would also have combined and continued to evolve from other swamps? Would it then not also be logical that the evolutionary process would have brought forth a variety of humanoids, or at least creatures with quite possibly our abilities or maybe more advanced? It seems that it would be highly unlikely that the process from different swamps would all evolve at the same pace and end up with the same result. Think about it; for example, if cells came together in a swamp on one of the American continents, and the same thing occurred on the European continent, would not the humans that evolved from these different swamps, in different parts of the world, be far more different than just different hair, eye or skin color? When we think of the possibility of life on other planets, we seldom assume they would be like us. We imagine little green 'men,' very different from us, yet beings growing out of different swamps tend to all end up the same.

The alternative to evolution is a single man and a single woman being created in a single location and a population then growing and spreading across the planet. Doesn't logic and reason point more toward the theory of a single pair of humans starting in a single location, than evolution or non-intelligent design?

Are you ready to accept that scientists could take a variety of single living cells, place them into a petri dish, and give them a billion years or so and *presto*, we would eventually have human beings or at least some rational, thinking being? To me, and I may be oversimplifying the concept, isn't it like taking all kinds of electronic components, placing them in a box, shaking them up, then just letting them be. Let's give them a billion years or so and over time, they might come together to become a computer. Computers may be pretty complex, yet nowhere near the complexity of human life, so can we explain human beings with this same oversimplified theory? We are expected to believe we grew from one single cell that just decided to divide into multiple cells and eventually evolve into us. Think about it. Can you really believe this to be a reasonable explanation?

We have all seen pictures of the chart showing the evolution of man from an ape-type creature on up to modern man. Simply looking at the chart, it almost makes sense, yet it begs the question: if we have evidence of thousands of ancient apes, and billions of 'modern' men, why do we find only one or two of these between stages, these so-called 'missing links'? This evolution process would have evolved so slowly over billions of years, and there would have to be tens of thousands, if not millions, of these various evolutionary stages. Where are they? Scientists who promote the theory of evolution get so excited when they find the one skeleton they want us to believe is evidence of a missing link in this evolutionary process. We have evidence of a vast number of ancient lives, such as all kinds of varieties of dinosaurs, and yet we find a single example of a missing link in the evolution of man. Does this make any kind of sense?

Do you find it believable that evolving from a single cell, over time, no matter how long that time may be, eventually evolved into a body, separating out cells to become muscle, bone, blood, as well as cells that would form organs, eyes that can see, ears that can hear, a brain that is capable of probably far more than we have yet to figure out? There clearly are scientists who find it easier to believe that scenario than to believe an intelligent being created us. Let your logic and reasoning prevail, then tell yourself which scenario is the most credible.

The universe is designed around specific laws of science, generally referred to as the laws of nature. Sound travels at a very precise speed, light travel at a precise speed, the human body functions at 98.6 degrees Fahrenheit. The list of specific laws that govern all of 'creation' cannot be random and would not have evolved by random chance. If it did, would there not be much more randomness to the 'laws of nature?'

Our bodies and certainly our brains are quite amazing, and it seems more so as we grow in knowledge and understanding of ourselves. It wasn't very long ago we discovered genes, DNA, and building blocks smaller than atoms. These unique bodies of ours have so many parts that all work together to function as the amazing creatures we are. The entire universe, the planets all work in a specific order and rotate in very specific patterns. Are you willing to accept all this as merely random chance?

One of the many mysteries of nature is the migration of the monarch butterfly. These butterflies begin heading south in September and October and travel from Canada and the United States to central Mexico, where they spend the winter months then begin to travel north again in March. No big deal, right? However, not a single butterfly that leaves the north to head to Mexico has ever been there before, and there are actually four generations between the time they start to migrate south and a year later when they do it all over again. Not a single butterfly has ever made the trek before, nor their parents or their parent's parents. So how can we account for the fact that they know exactly when and where to go and when and where to return to? This is not totally unique; nature is full of these kinds of occurrences, making chance or random evolution a hard sell when it comes to explaining these types of phenomena.

Over time, we came to understand that the planets do not revolve around the Earth and that the Earth is not flat; we can transplant human organs, and maybe we are just scratching the surface of what else we will be able to do one day. Is it possible that one day we might, in our wisdom, also conclude that as smart as we may be, we may not be the smartest of all beings, that maybe—just maybe—there is a God who put this all in motion and continues to watch over all of His creation?

Albert Einstein once said, "the more I study science, the more I believe in God." Charles Hard Townes, the 1964 Nobel Prize winner in physics and the founder of laser science, said, "I strongly believe in the existence of God, based on intuition, observation, logic and scientific knowledge." I could fill a chapter with quotes from some of the most brilliant minds throughout our history who feel that the only explanation of science is God. I ask you to continue to examine the facts rather than relying on the reasoning of others. The wisdom of those scientists may be compelling, but in the end, it has to be your logical conclusions that matter.

Pick up a Bible, read Genesis' description of creation; God spoke everything into existence. Doesn't the Big Bang theory sound a lot like creation as described in Genesis, everything coming into existence in a single instant by the will of an intelligent designer? Does it really make more sense to say it was all created by itself from nothing? How can we explain something from nothing and anything having a beginning if there was no one to create the first particle, the first building blocks of the universe?

I cannot prove beyond a reasonable doubt that God exists any more than anyone else can prove beyond a reasonable doubt that God *does not* exist, but looking at all the evidence, it certainly seems that logic and reasoning would lead us toward intelligent design over random evolution. I hear nature screaming intelligent design, God!

CHAPTER 2
Why Jesus?

Why should you accept that Jesus Christ is the Son of God? Why should you believe that the only path to salvation, and ultimately heaven, is by faith in Jesus Christ?

First of all, because He said so. In the Gospel of John, Jesus, speaking to a man named Nicodemus, told him no one could enter the kingdom unless he was 'born again.' On another occasion, Jesus said, "no one comes to the Father except through me." Over and over again, Jesus made it clear that He was the ONLY path to heaven. He never said the road to heaven has many paths and following me just *might* be one of them. He could not have made that point any clearer.

Before we get too far, I have to assume that you have not yet accepted that Jesus Christ is the Son of God and that you have to follow Him and only Him if you are not going to end up in hell. You may be 'sort of' leaning toward believing, yet you still have doubts. You may be asking yourself, "If I'm not sure He is who he says He is, how can I assume what He says is also true and that the Bible is reliable?" I will address the reliability of the Bible in the next chapter.

You may not believe all that you have read so far, but bear with me, at least for now, and be willing to consider that all of it just might be true. If you continue reading through the following chapters, you may have gathered enough evidence to come to some conclusions. But, once again, for now, just keep an open mind.

I know that believing Jesus and certainly believing there is no way to heaven except by faith in Him flies in the face of the secular world view. The world propagates a lot of untruths. The world would have you accept that if you choose to believe there is a God, there has to be more than one path that leads to Him, and you can decide to choose your own path. After all, don't all paths—Hinduism, Judaism, Islam, or any of the other religions— all lead to God? So why choose to believe in this Jesus? What makes Him so special?

Did Jesus really exist? Is His existence only verified in the Bible, a book that you are not sure you can trust? The answer to the first question is yes, the second is no. There is a lot of non-biblical evidence regarding Jesus. Literally, billions of people around the globe believe Jesus was one of the most important figures in world history, yet at the same time, there are certainly large numbers of people that don't believe He existed at all. The reality is that it is not about the numbers. I am not telling you to believe because a lot of other people do. I am asking you to hear me out, hear the evidence, examine the evidence, then make your own decision.

A survey conducted by the Church of England in 2015 revealed 22 percent of adults in England did not believe Jesus was a real person.[2] Lawrence Mykytiuk, an associate professor of library science at Purdue University and author of a 2015 *Biblical Archaeology Review* article on the extra-biblical evidence of Jesus, notes there was no debate about the issue in ancient times. He said, "Jewish rabbis who did not like Jesus or His followers accused Him of being a magician and leading people astray, but they never said He didn't exist."[3]

Archeologically, there is very little, if any, real evidence that can irrefutably verify His existence, but the same can be said about the majority of people living at the time, at least peasant people. A king or someone of worldly significance might leave an archaeological trail, but like most of us common 'folk,' two thousand years from now, archaeological evidence of our existence will probably be nonexistent as well.

There are items like the crown of thorns, believed by many to be the 'crown of thorns' worn by Jesus, housed in the Cathedral of Notre Dame in Paris (and actually survived the devastating fire of

2019), but there is nothing that can verify that it was worn to the cross by Jesus. There is the Shroud of Turin, which is believed by many to be the burial cloth of Jesus. Carbon dating done on the shroud tends to disprove its authenticity, yet many Christians still choose to believe these items are indeed actual artifacts attributable to Jesus. But clearly, since Jesus did not live in a palace or have worldly riches, there is little or no real physical evidence left behind. The largest body of evidence is the lack of anyone disputing His existence at the time His followers were preaching His death and resurrection. There were those who did not witness the risen Jesus who may have questioned the resurrection, but no one denied His existence, and there were thousands who witnessed His life.

There is a significant amount of non-biblical documentation regarding the existence of Jesus. The first-century Jewish historian Flavius Josephus is probably our best source of information about first-century Palestine. Josephus twice mentions Jesus in his 20-volume history of the Jewish people written around 93 A.D.

Josephus was believed to have been born around 37 A.D., a few years after the crucifixion of Jesus. He was a well-connected aristocrat and military leader in Palestine who served as a commander in Galilee during the First Jewish Revolt against Rome between 66 and 70 A.D. Josephus was not a follower of Jesus, but he was around when the early church was getting started, so he knew people who had seen and heard Jesus.

In one passage of Josephus' history, he writes about an unlawful execution and identifies the victim as James, the brother of Jesus, who is called Messiah. Few scholars doubt the authenticity of the account.

Another account of Jesus appears in *Annals of Imperial Rome*, a first-century history of the Roman Empire written around 116 A.D. by the Roman senator and historian Tacitus. In chronicling the burning of Rome in 64 A.D., Tacitus mentions that Emperor Nero falsely blamed "the persons commonly called Christians, who were hated for their enormities. Christus, the founder of the name, was put to death by Pontius Pilate, procurator of Judea in the reign of Tiberius."[4]

As a Roman historian, Tacitus did not have any Christian biases in his discussion of the persecution of Christians by Nero. Nearly everything Tacitus says coincides with what the New Testament itself says: Jesus was executed by the governor of Judea, Pontius Pilate, for crimes against the state, and a religious movement of his followers sprang up in His wake.

When Tacitus wrote history, anytime he considered the information not entirely reliable, he generally wrote some indication of that for his readers, but there is no such indication of potential error in the passage that mentions Jesus. Shortly before Tacitus wrote his account of Jesus, Roman governor Pliny the Younger wrote to Emperor Trajan that early Christians would "sing hymns to Christ as to a god." Some scholars also believe Roman historian Suetonius references Jesus in noting that Emperor Claudius had expelled Jews from Rome who "were making constant disturbances at the instigation of Chrestus."

We don't find a lot of information about Jesus in any of these historical writings, but it is certainly clear that Jesus was known by historians who had reason to look into the matter. No one ever thought or suggested He was made up or didn't really exist. We don't have to accept Jesus' existence strictly on faith or just because the Bible says so. There is adequate evidence in history to support His existence and His death by crucifixion.

I have shared a lot regarding the existence of Jesus, but we need to look at the *why* of Jesus as well. In Chapter 5, I will discuss the concept of salvation, but I need to at least touch on it here since the *why* is all about salvation. We are taught that God became man for one reason: to substitute Himself on the cross to atone for the sins of mankind, absolutely true. However, I believe there were other reasons as well. At least one of the reasons was to help us to better connect with Him. Until God became man, taking on human flesh as Jesus Christ, we had never seen God. Throughout history, God communicated with us in various ways, but since God is not a physical being and had no earthly, human body, we never saw Him. For thousands of years, we only heard from this God through prophets, visits by angels (messengers) and verbally as He spoke to men like Adam, Noah and Moses, to name just a few. (The English word *angel* comes from the Greek word *angelos* and means *messenger*.)

When I think of God, I picture Jesus based on what He looked like in the mind of all the artist renditions of what they believed He may have looked like. So, by becoming man, Jesus gave us a real-life visual, someone that looked like us, someone that we could begin to understand and relate to and even have a relationship with.

I believe it was important for God to become man for another reason. We now had a face, maybe just an artist's rendition of the face of the real Jesus, but a face just the same. We could no longer come to Him and say, "but God, you don't understand what it's like to be me; you can't really understand what I'm going through. You just don't know what it's like to be a human." He chose to arrive in the world at a time in human history when day-to-day living was not easy. It was a time when there were no conveniences at all; no running water, no paved streets, and homes that, by today's standards, we might not consider habitable. He experienced all of the things that each of us experience: sadness, joy, hunger, and pain. He got tired, even exhausted just like any of us and then He suffered more pain than we could ever imagine. So, mankind can never again come before God to tell Him He just doesn't understand; believe me, He does!

As Jesus breathed his last breath on the cross with the words, "it is finished," His purpose on earth had been completed, the work that His Father sent Him to do was done. The relationship between God and man was forever changed; He had paid the price for our salvation in full and opened the door for all of mankind to have a personal relationship with their Creator.

CHAPTER 3

Can We Trust the Bible?

I have covered the historical evidence of the existence of Jesus as a person, but since all support for the divinity of Jesus is entirely based on Biblical accounts, we have to take a good look to determine if we can rely on the authenticity of these Biblical accounts.

I believe the Bible is the Word of God and that Almighty God inspired each of the 'authors' to write all 66 books contained in the Bible. There will always be those who argue or attempt to prove errors and inconsistencies in the Bible; there are none. However, it is necessary to define the term errors when we are speaking of the Bible. The Bible is not the work of divine dictation; God did not dictate the Bible word-for-word to its authors. If He had, we would have to conclude that there would be absolutely no error, as each word would be His word. This is not the case, and there is a distinct difference between dictation and inspiration. I had said earlier there were no errors in the Bible, and I am sure there are theologians who will cringe at what I am about to say. Loosely stated, and I do mean loosely defined, one could argue that there are errors. This may sound like I am talking in circles and actually contradicting myself. Let me explain. As I said, the Bible is not the work of dictation, but instead, it was inspired by God. God inspired each author to document events and teachings and did not provide the authors with a word-for-word dictation.

The result is that certain events, such as two occasions where Jesus multiplied a few fish and loaves to feed thousands of followers, may contain 'minor' inaccuracies that have no effect on the essence of the events described. One occasion places the number at 4,000, and on another occasion, there were 5,000. These were two distinctly separate occasions. Were there exactly 4,000 on one of those occasions and 5,000 at the other? Probably not, but the fact that Jesus fed a large multitude numbering in the thousands on both of these occasions with only a small amount of fish and loaves of bread is factual and is clearly a real event that God inspired the writer to document. The description of the miracle of multiplying fish and loaves to feed thousands is no less factual nor is it inaccurate or in error even though the number of loaves may not be exact nor the headcount of the followers who were fed. The fact remains that though the numbers may or may not be absolutely accurate does not mean the Bible is riddled with errors and thereby is incapable of being the Word of God. If God had determined that the exact numbers had any real significance, He certainly would have assured an accurate accounting of the people as well as the fish and loaves. The point is: the numbers are totally irrelevant.

Jesus often taught using parables. For example, in the Gospel of Matthew, Chapter 25, Jesus tells a story of the ten virgins, five having enough oil for their lamps, and five not having enough. Was this an actual event? Most likely not; it was a teaching regarding being prepared for Christ's return. Another Gospel mentions a miracle where two men were healed by Jesus, while another Gospel account of what appears to be the same event mentions only one. Once again, the miracle and the event happened, and it is described in two of the Gospels by two separate writers. Whether the healing was of two men or one doesn't make the Gospels in conflict with each other, as the event is what matters, not the number of men whose sight was restored. These are the types of 'inconsistencies' that have been pointed out as 'errors' by those who would like to delegitimize scripture. To be absolutely clear, the Bible does not contain errors or conflicts when it comes to documenting actual events nor in Jesus' teachings.

The Bible, as we know it, of course, did not always exist in its current format. The Bible contains 66 books, 39 in the Old Testament and 27 in the New Testament. The Old Testament of the Christian Bible contains the 39 books known as the Jewish Tanakh;

the name stands for the original promise of God to the descendants of Abraham. It covers the period from creation up to about 433 years before the birth of Christ. The New Testament starts at the birth of Christ, or a period immediately preceding His birth in some of the Gospels. Somewhere near the end of the fourth century, the current 27 books of the New Testament were painstakingly studied and reviewed by a large group of Biblical scholars, who determined that these Gospel accounts and letters were deemed to be God-inspired and to be considered the entirety of the New Testament.

Many other works had been reviewed for consideration but were not included. Some will contend that they were eliminated because they didn't 'fit' the 'story,' or contradicted the narrative the church wanted to present. Actually, they were eliminated from inclusion because they clearly did contradict documents that were irrefutably determined to be God's inspired word. The large number of examiners involved and the diversity of those doing the review did so without any agenda other than seeking truth. Many of these disallowed texts have been looked at over the centuries, and no evidence was ever found to suggest they were inspired or should have been included. If we are to accept the Bible as being God-inspired, it would be foolish to think the process of elimination and inclusion would not also be inspired by God. God certainly would have guided the process of weeding out the documents that He had not inspired.

The New Testament consists of the four Gospels documenting the life of Jesus along with the 23 letters written to various early Christian individuals or congregations by authors such as Paul, John, James, Peter, and others, as well as some whose authorship is uncertain. The Gospels are attributed to have been written by Matthew, Mark, Luke, and John. Everything in these accounts of the life of Jesus was written by those who either saw the events with their own eyes or recorded other first-hand accounts of the life and teachings of and actual words spoken by Jesus. The book of James, as well as the book of Jude in the New Testament, were written by two men who just happened to be Jesus' half-brothers, who certainly qualify as having first-hand knowledge of Jesus. Still, how do we know they are factual accounts to be trusted, and should we believe Jesus did indeed rise from the dead? Acceptance that Jesus was raised from the dead is central to Christianity. Without it, Christianity fails to be anything but a fairy tale.

Let's start with Jesus' apostles, a ragtag bunch of guys Jesus called to follow him along His three-year journey of preaching and teaching, a journey eventually leading to His death and, most importantly, His resurrection. To add a little perspective, in the Jewish culture of the day, most young Jewish boys dreamed of being called by a rabbi to be a disciple. The rabbis called those who were thought to be the best and brightest to be their disciples, and they eventually would become rabbis themselves. Those who were not called had to seek other ways of making a living. For young Jewish men, this often-meant manual labor like fishing, carpentry, or some other trade. When Jesus started to call His disciples, He was calling those who had not been chosen by any of the other rabbis, and many had been fishermen.

The word disciple means follower or pupil, and the literal Hebrew meaning was 'to walk in one's dust,' meaning they were expected to follow so closely they actually were walking in the dust of the rabbis' footsteps. Jesus' disciples were no different; these men followed Him virtually day and night throughout His three-year ministry. They were with Him when He drew thousands to hear Him speak; they saw Him raise people from the dead; they were there when He healed the sick by the thousands, changed water to wine, and fed thousands with a few loaves of bread and a few fish. They saw Him walk on water, calm the seas, and truly came to believe that He was the Messiah, the Son of God.

Although Jesus had warned them of what was coming, it certainly seemed as if they never fully understood it until after the resurrection. During their time with Him, they heard His words, they saw the miracles, and yet, they believed at least somewhat like the rest of the Jewish nation—that the promised Messiah would be different. They still believed He would rise up and start His kingdom here on earth, overthrowing the Roman domination of their people. There is speculation that Judas, the disciple who sold Jesus for thirty pieces of silver, did so to force His hand, believing that if He was arrested, He would then have no choice but to use His divinity to rise up against the Romans, freeing Israel and become King. We will never really know Judas' motives, but needless to say, whatever they were, they were clearly evil and self-serving.

Some 750 years before Jesus' birth, it was prophesied that a Messiah would be sent to the nation of Israel. They believed this promised Messiah would be like Moses, who led them out of Egyptian bondage. Most Jews failed to accept Jesus as the Messiah since He did not fit the image of the Messiah they believed was to come, someone who would free His people from Roman bondage. They never understood that the bondage the Messiah was coming to save them from was the bondage of sin.

When Jesus was arrested, tried, and sentenced to death, the apostles, His closest friends and followers, went into panic mode, and as they watched Jesus actually die on the cross, they really began to panic. How could this man, whom they believed was the Son of God, die? How could He create a kingdom if He was dead? They were scared and confused, but what they did know for sure was that they could be the next to die. Certainly, if the Romans killed their leader, they would come after His followers next. They immediately went into hiding. On the night Jesus was arrested, Peter, who was Jesus' 'right-hand man,' denied, not once, but three times that he knew Jesus.

One thing is certain, there is no way these terrified men would think about preaching the teachings of Jesus to the world. At this point, all they wanted to do was to hide, maybe go back to their old jobs, blend in, and get on with their lives. They were in shock and were totally demoralized. Yet all of a sudden, they began to preach, not only Jesus' teachings, but the good news of a risen Lord, and no matter what threats came their way, they could not and would not be silenced.

Sometime after seeing the risen Christ, Peter, the man who denied knowing Jesus, had been thrown into prison along with some of the other apostles for proclaiming the resurrection. When they were released, they were told to stop their proclamation. Peter said he could not, and if he remained silent, the very stones would shout out. These previously terrified men had now seen the risen Christ, and they would never remain silent again.

So, what changed? Upon seeing Jesus after He had risen from the dead, their faith had been fully restored, and it would never again be shaken. They knew that no matter how badly their faith may have been shaken in the past, all doubt was gone; Jesus had died and rose again, and there could no longer be any doubt that He was the Son of God. They were now willing to be beaten, threatened, imprisoned, and eventually die for what they knew to be the truth.

I found the following account of how some of the apostles/disciples died, but I cannot verify the absolute accuracy of this account as there are some other minor variations in other accounts, but it is known they did die brutal deaths for proclaiming their faith in the risen Christ.

- Matthew suffered martyrdom in Ethiopia, killed by a sword wound.
- Mark was dragged by horses through the streets until he was dead.
- Luke was hanged in Greece.
- John faced martyrdom when he was boiled in a huge basin of boiling oil during a wave of persecution in Rome. However, he was miraculously delivered from death. He was then sentenced to the mines on the prison Island of Patmos. He died an old man, the only apostle to die peacefully.
- Peter was crucified upside down on an X-shaped cross.
- James, Jesus' half-brother, the leader of the church in Jerusalem, was thrown over a hundred feet down from the southeast pinnacle of the Temple when he refused to deny his faith in Christ. He survived the fall and then was beaten to death with a club.
- James, the Son of Zebedee, was beheaded at Jerusalem. The Roman officer who guarded James watched amazed as James defended his faith at his trial. The officer walked beside James to the place of execution. Overcome by conviction, he declared his new faith to the judge and knelt beside James to accept beheading as a Christian.
- Bartholomew, also known as Nathaniel, was flayed to death by a whip.
- Andrew was crucified on an X-shaped cross in Patras, Greece. After being whipped severely by seven soldiers, they tied his body to the cross with cords to prolong his ag-

ony. He continued to preach to his tormentors for two days until he finally died.

- Thomas was stabbed with a spear in India.
- Jude was killed with arrows when he refused to deny his faith in Christ.
- Matthias, the apostle chosen to replace the traitor Judas Iscariot, was stoned and then beheaded.
- Paul was tortured and then beheaded by the evil Emperor Nero at Rome in 67 A.D. He endured a lengthy imprisonment, which allowed him to write his many letters to the churches he had formed throughout the Roman Empire. These letters, which taught many of the foundations and doctrines of Christianity, form a large portion of the New Testament.

Do you believe for a second these men would have been willing to die for Jesus had He not proved to them that He had actually risen from the dead? Do you think they would have been willing to die for a hoax? What could they possibly have gained by it? Put yourself in their shoes; can you imagine dying for a lie? Making a choice to die for the truth is not a choice any of us would find easy to make, let alone a lie. Most of us will never have to face that kind of choice, and fortunately, Jesus only asks us to live for Him, not to die for Him. But that doesn't mean that Christians are not facing death for their faith in Jesus Christ virtually every day in places like China, North Korea, Sudan, Iran and in much of the Middle East.

Think about this: when the teachings of Jesus and His resurrection was being preached by his followers and documented in writing, there were literally tens of thousands still alive who had witnessed many of the events. Would there not have been a huge backlash from those who witnessed these events if what was being preached wasn't true? There is no record anywhere, dating back to the time of the gospels, that contradicts a single event. To me, that speaks volumes as to the accuracy of the gospels. Jesus also said to His disciples before He left to return to Heaven, "I will send you the Holy Spirit who will teach you and remind you of what I have said."

I believe the accuracy and authenticity of the New Testament for all the reasons I have just described. My support for the authenticity of the Old Testament is based on the thousands of years that the Jewish people have unequivocally accepted it to be the Word of their God and the fact that Jesus Himself often quoted from it.

Charles Colson, a principal character in the Watergate scandal of the Nixon era, is quoted as saying, "I know the resurrection is a fact, and Watergate proved it to me. How? Because twelve men testified they had seen Jesus raised from the dead, then they proclaimed that truth for forty years, never once denying it. Every one was beaten, tortured, stoned and put in prison. They would not have endured that if it weren't true. Watergate embroiled twelve of the most powerful men in the world and they couldn't keep a lie for three weeks. You're telling me twelve apostles could keep a lie for forty years? Absolutely impossible."[5]

Best-selling author Lee Strobel said, "I went to a psychologist friend and said if 500 people claimed to see Jesus after he died, it was just a hallucination. He said hallucinations are an individual event. If 500 people have the same hallucination, that's a bigger miracle than the resurrection."[6]

We so often hear about archaeological findings that verify the existence of sites described in the Bible that had never been known to exist except in Biblical references. Over time, archeology has verified many Biblical sites, yet not a single discovery has ever disproved a single line of scripture. In 2019, archeologists believe they had located what they believe to be the town of Emmaus mentioned in the New Testament. Maybe not a major event, but these kinds of discoveries have occurred many times over the past century. Just more evidence of authenticity when it comes to Biblical references.

At this point, if you are still not ready to accept the Bible as absolute truth, you have to at least give serious consideration to the fact that there certainly is a lot of evidence pointing to its truth.

The Bible is not an à la carte document, you cannot pick and choose which books or chapters or verses you want to accept as truth and ignore the rest. The Bible is the Word of God, or it is not. It is that simple. You can choose to devalue it to the word of man, or you can accept it as God's Word. That is the beauty of choice, of free will; you get to decide, but you need to decide based on reason and logic, not preconceived notions or ideas.

CHAPTER 4

Do You Need to Study the Bible?

The answer is yes, you do indeed need to study the Bible. The Bible is not a novel to be read; it is a manual to be studied.

Billy Graham, a man whom I believe to be the Godliest man of my lifetime, once said, "read the Bible with expectancy, it's an interview with almighty God." He also said we should expect that every time we pick up the Bible, God has a message for us. "The Holy Spirit inspired the writing of this book, and the Holy Spirit can interpret this book for us."

The Bible is the single source for you to find God's plan for your life as well as a pathway to the next. The most common tool for how to do practically anything today is YouTube. Literally, millions of people search YouTube every day to find out how to do virtually anything from replacing a kitchen faucet to repairing your computer. It is an awesome resource, and if it had been around in the first century, Matthew, Mark, Luke, and John, as well as Peter, James, and Paul might have used it to share the message of salvation. I don't know if God is or is not a fan of social media and if He would have chosen to use it, had it been available 2,000 years ago. I'm also not suggesting that social media is inherently evil either, but it sure seems that a lot of evil gets spewed by way of an anonymous internet. It never ceases to amaze me when I read the kind of things people will post when they can hide in anonymity. But the fact is, it was not available to Jesus or the apostles, so instead, God chose to provide us with a single document written by a multitude of authors, directly inspired by Him to be our very own 'how-to' manual.

Most of us do not spend a lot of time thinking about eternity; it's just one of those somewhat vague concepts, and we tend to spend most of our effort dealing with the here and now. We just kind of forget to give much, if any, thought to what comes after this life. I know that this life can sometimes feel like an eternity to us and especially when things are not going well. But as long as this life may seem, even if we live a very long life, it is nothing. In the Book of James in the New Testament, James, the half-brother of Jesus, tells us that our lives are nothing more than a mist, here one minute and gone the next.

To help us put a little perspective on eternity, think about this. I once read or heard this somewhere (don't remember where), but if a bird came once every day and rubbed his beak on the world's tallest mountain, by the time the bird had worn the entire mountain totally away, eternity will have just begun. If you accept the possibility of God and an afterlife, our time here is inconsequential when compared to eternity. However, that does not mean that it is meaningless or of no value. Our time here, no matter how short or long it may be, sets the stage for the next. What we do here determines where we will spend eternity. God did not want us spending this very important time without direction, a ship without a rudder drifting aimlessly in the sea of life. We needed a 'how-to' to navigate this life in light of the next. The Bible is the answer. It is our rudder and our GPS, if we choose to use it. The Bible tells us to live life in the light of eternity, meaning everything you do should involve consideration as to how it will affect where you will spend eternity.

For us, eternity is difficult to comprehend. Everything we know is based on time. We live in seconds, minutes, hours, days and even years; eternity, endlessness, lack of time, is a term that is so very hard to wrap our heads around. I've heard it said that God lives strictly in the present. For God, there is no time, nothing happens in the past or the future; forever is a now that never ends.

Most people, when asked if they study the Bible and even some who consider themselves to be Christians, will answer, "I have tried to, but it is so hard to read" or "I have tried, but I just don't understand most of it." I don't believe for a minute that God intended the Bible, His Word, to be something that would have to be interpreted by Biblical scholars and theologians. Now, these scholars certainly can help us in any study of the Bible, but know this, it was written directly to you and me individually. God had you directly in mind when He inspired this book. As Billy Graham said, it is a love letter from God to you! He also said, "it is an interview with God." It is not intended to be mysterious; it is not full of riddles you may or may not be able to figure out. The Bible is your personal letter from God. If there is anything 'magical' (and I hate to use that term, but for this thought, it seems appropriate), it is the fact that it is so personal and timeless. It was never intended to be written exclusively for those living at the time it was written; it is a timeless document. Nothing in it applies to those living thousands of years ago that isn't still completely relevant for our lives today. Over thousands of years, the world certainly has changed but the beauty of the Bible is that the Word of God has never changed and never will. Isn't it reassuring to know that there is at least one stable, unchanging thing that we can always count on?

God is not going to rewrite the Bible for our generation. We need to stop trying to change the scripture that was written to change us. We spend so much time trying to bend and twist scripture to meet our beliefs instead of trying to conform our lives to God's. God gave us His Word to help shape and guide us, not for us to select the portions we like so we can shape our vision of God. God created man in His image, yet man keeps trying to shape God into his image.

You cannot read the Bible, then say, "OK, I've read the Bible." Study it with the knowledge and understanding that it is your link to God, and it will speak directly to you in a way that only God can. Its content will be made known to you and you will hear exactly what God wants you to hear when God wants and needs you to hear it, but only as long your heart and mind are open to Him.

From the very beginning, God's plan was for you to have a personal relationship with Him, and there is no other way for you to get close to Him and have that relationship without getting to know Him. You may not be able to see Him or actually hear his voice, at least out loud, but He can and does still communicate with you. The only way you can get to know Him is by studying His Word. God's word is your direct link to Him. If you want to know what He said, look to the Bible; if you want to know what He wants for you, look to the Bible.

I cannot tell you how often I have heard people say they believe they will go to heaven, but at the same time, if asked what Jesus said you must do to get to heaven, they don't know. It is no different from assuming you can do brain surgery having never studied it, never earned a degree in medicine or especially surgery, but you heard about it and maybe saw a brain surgery performed on TV once. Brain surgery is probably one of the most difficult and complex surgeries, so one would think that it might take a little more than having heard about it to pull it off successfully. Where you end up for all eternity is a lot more critical than brain surgery so having heard about God, having heard about His Word, just might not be enough to ensure that you will get to heaven. If you expect or at least want to go to heaven when you die, it might be a good idea to hear what God has to say about how to do it.

A devotional published in *In Touch Daily Readings for Devoted Living*, on June 20, 2019, seems to underscore this very point.

> *In the 1990s, many Christians joined the trend of wearing small wristbands bearing the letters W.W.J.D. which stood for the question "What Would Jesus Do?" Although the fad has passed, the question is still valid. It's designed to prompt us to consider whether our words, actions, and attitudes are an accurate reflection of the life of our Savior.*[7]

However, before we can accurately assess whether we are doing what Jesus would do, we need to have a comprehensive understanding of what He said and did, as recorded in Scripture. It's easy to take a few verses and come away with a simplistic view of the Lord. Most people are tempted to make Jesus into an image of what they want Him to be instead of trying to see the whole picture. Yes, He responded to people with love and compassion, but He also told them to stop sinning and warned them about the dangers of hell.

How can you begin to follow a Jesus you don't really know? You can only come to know Him by studying what He said and did, and you can't 'cherry-pick' by finding a verse that you like or want to take out of context. You must have a complete and total understanding of Him to know what He expects and wants from you. Jesus wants you to come to Him, and the most direct path to Him is through a study of His scripture.

Today, we see a lot of 'cherry-picking' from scripture, often used to try to add credence to falsehoods. We allow social media to convince us of the validity of some of these falsehoods. If we read it on one of these social media platforms, it must be true. Social media is not the place to look for truth. I clearly am not saying the opposite either; I am not saying that everything on social media is a lie, but read with discernment.

On June 26, 2000, ABC aired a documentary called, *Peter Jennings Reporting: Finding Jesus.* It was advertised as "a journalist's exploration of the historical figure of Jesus. This fascinating documentary provides extensive insights into the 2,000-year-old story of Christianity and the man whose life continues to inspire devotion and debate." I watched it back in 2000 and came away with only one conclusion: if I wanted to find Jesus, Peter Jennings was not going to be my source. I would certainly hope you have seen and read enough on social media and in print media and heard on TV and radio, that you are aware that only a fraction of what is out there is 'real,' is truthful, and is not heavily biased.

We all have some kind of bias based on our beliefs and understandings, and not unexpectedly, we tend to embrace reporting that leans toward our personal bias. You already know all of the media has a bias so you will go to the one that aligns itself with your bias. That is perfectly normal and natural. When you look to the Bible, don't look for what you want to hear; look for what God wants you to hear. Once again, leave your bias at the door; open the Bible expecting unbiased truth because that is what you will discover.

If you wanted to get to know some of our founding fathers, you would certainly read things they had written as well as some biographies, and you would get a pretty good idea of what they were like, how they thought, and what they intended when they wrote; for example, the Constitution. Some Constitutional scholars believe you need to know the framers' background, their thoughts,

and their beliefs on various topics to understand what was intended when they wrote the Constitution. Some believe that the Constitution has to be interpreted with that kind of background and
understanding of what the framers were thinking when they wrote
it. There are also those, such as the late Antonin Scalia, who believed that what they might have been thinking had no bearing on
interpretation. Scalia believed that what they wrote alone matters
and you must not attempt to read into it.

Scalia's view may or may not be appropriate for the interpretation of the Constitution, but it cannot be applied to Scripture. Our
founding fathers, the framers of our Constitution, never intended for you to one day develop a personal relationship with any of
them. But God intended for you to develop a personal relationship
with Him. God wants you to get to know Him so intimately that
there can be no misunderstanding of His intentions. The Bible
does not directly address every single issue that will ever come up
in your lifetime. Knowing right and wrong sometimes requires an
intimate knowledge of Him to find the answers. Let me use this
example; you may have an issue that you and your spouse have
never discussed, yet you know your spouse so well, you have total
confidence as to what your spouse would say or feel on an issue.
That is a compelling reason for the kind of personal relationship
God wants with us. WWJD, that I spoke of earlier, has no meaning
if you have no idea what Jesus would do and you can only know
from having the kind of close personal relationship that He seeks
to have with you.

For example, Jesus never spoke against slavery, never directly
addressed abortion, never directly addressed homosexuality, so
shall we then assume a blanket approval? Although Jesus did not
speak directly on some of these issues, keep in mind that the Bible
is God's word, and the Bible does clearly address some of these.
Should we assume everything He did not address is, by default,
OK? Regardless of your position on these and many more issues,
you cannot equate silence with approval. When you know God,
when you truly know Jesus, He will speak to your heart and you
will know His heart. When you choose to know His will, He will
provide all the direction and answers you desire. Seeking guidance
through prayer will always bring answers. Don't ask for confirma-

tion of your opinions; ask for help in knowing His.

You may wonder why there are four Gospels chronicling the life of Jesus. Couldn't He have had one author detail His life? Here is my explanation. I liken it to an NFL game on TV. The networks could get by using a single camera, and you could say you saw the game, but by using a multitude of cameras, you not only get to see the game, but on TV, your view will be better than actually sitting in the stands, even the very expensive box seats or suites. Jesus chose to use four writers who would allow you to 'see' Jesus from four different perspectives, much like the different cameras showing you what's happening on the field during a football game. And unlike those who sat on the hillside 2,000 years ago to hear Jesus, you have instant replay. You can read it over and over again, and much like instant replay, each time you read a portion of the Bible, God may choose to show you something you may have missed the previous times. I cannot tell you how many times I have read the Bible, and yet nearly every time I come across something, a light goes on, and I find myself understanding something I didn't get in any of the previous readings.

When you study the Bible, the Holy Spirit will open your mind and heart to what you need to hear. Over time, you will come to know Jesus, drawing nearer to Him each time. Each person will learn what God wants them to learn and what He wants them to hear. When we speak of doctrine, I am not suggesting that there will be different right and wrong for each reader. There is only one truth, but how God gets that message to each of us will vary as we study the same Bible. Truth is truth, there is not your truth and my truth; there is only God's truth, and it never changes. It hasn't changed over the centuries and it never will. We are all different and we are all dealing with different issues in this life of ours, and God may need to speak to you about something He doesn't need to speak to me about, and you will hear a message from a passage that I don't get.

It is like two people sitting side by side in church on a Sunday morning listening to a pastor's message; one walks out, thinking God really spoke to him while the other got nothing from the message. Or, two children grow up in the same household with the same parents, and having been treated and taught the same, turn out so very differently. We are all different, and that is why God speaks to us differently, and that is how God can use the same words in the same Bible to tell very different people just what they need to hear.

If you merely read the Bible rather than study it, you will come up short. The link between God and man is the written word. Jesus is no longer walking the earth; He left us with His Word and the Holy Spirit to help guide us through it.

The only way you can know the truth of God's teachings is to study His word. The only way you can get to know Him is to study His Word, and He does want you to know Him and wants you to draw near to Him. If you want to get to know God, you need to spend time with Him.

CHAPTER 5
Salvation from What?

If you have already accepted that there is a God, or if you are at least considering the possibility that there is a God, you may be ready for the next step; the possibility that Jesus just may be who He said He was, the Son of God. You may very well be asking yourself, why do I have to make a choice or a decision about any of it? The answer is because your salvation depends on it. Then the next obvious question is, what is salvation and what is it I need saving from?

Likely, salvation is not a word that crosses your mind very often, if ever. Most of us don't think about the need for salvation because even if you did think about heaven and hell, you certainly aren't sure what the process is to avoid hell and eventually end up in heaven. You may not give much thought at all to eternity. After all, death, heaven, hell, eternity; these are all things that are a long way off. The reality is that it just may be a lot closer than you want to think about. People die every day, and guess what? More often than not, it happens to those who were not expecting it. Read the obituaries; not all of those who die are old. We all hope for long lives, but it can all come to an end in an instant.

If you believe the Biblical account of creation, you know that the God who created all things created man and woman and placed them in the Garden of Eden, an earthly paradise. God told them they had dominion over all of His creation. He gave them a single rule, which they soon broke, committing the first sin. This sin would separate God and man forever because the first sin would not be the last. We are all the descendants of these fallen ancestors. The result for mankind was expulsion from the garden. God told them that from that point forward, life would be difficult. No matter how good or bad our lives may be, we certainly have to admit that it is no Garden of Paradise. We all experience hardships, suffer illness, pain and eventual death, none of which these first two humans would have endured if they had simply chosen to obey God.

The Bible tells us the first sin was eating from the tree of good and evil. Satan found it easy to temp man by telling them eating from the tree of good and evil would make them as smart as God. How could they resist? They ate from the single forbidden tree, and yes, they now knew evil. There was no evil in the world God had created, but Satan quickly changed all that and now had a foothold. From that point on, as you might expect, sinning just got a lot easier. When you ask what do we need saving from, the answer is generally ourselves, mostly because no one makes us choose evil over good. Warren W. Wiersbe, in his book titled *"Wiersbe's Expository Outlines on the New Testament,"* said, "God sends trials to bring out the best in us, but Satan sends temptations to bring out the worst."[8] I need to be very clear on this issue; God does not tempt us; God does not send evil. He does, however, allow evil or life's trials to strengthen us. It is "the evil one" who temps us and we only have ourselves to blame when we choose poorly. We need salvation because there isn't a single one of us who have not sinned; therefore, we are all in need of forgiveness.

In the preface, I mentioned the term 'born-again' and told you I would explain just what the term means. In the Gospel of John, chapter 3, Jesus told a man named Nicodemus that man must be born-again if he is to enter the kingdom of God. And Nicodemus' response was, "how can a man be born again when he is an adult?" The term means to become a new person in Christ. To assure salvation, we have to be able to remove the punishment we 'earned' as a result of our sin, and it can only be removed by the grace and mercy of Jesus Christ. We can call God's justice punishment or discipline, but clearly, when we separate ourselves from God and turn from Him, punishment is what we have earned. God disciplines us, hoping to help us choose to change our lives, but if we refuse, we can certainly expect punishment.

Mercy is defined as not getting what we deserve, and *grace* is getting something we do not deserve. We deserve punishment for sinning, yet God's mercy offers us the opportunity to have the punishment removed and, in the eyes of God, to become as pure as the day we were conceived. Through the grace of God, Jesus freely chose to go to the cross in our place, paying the price for our sins. By making a commitment to change our lives, turn away from sin, accept Jesus as the Christ, the Son of God, and simply ask for His forgiveness, we are made clean. This rebirth that happens when we welcome Jesus into our lives is the definition of being born-again. Salvation opens the door to heaven for everyone willing to accept the gift.

Salvation will not automatically turn you into a *perfect* human. Born-again Christians sin, but when you make the born-again commitment, you begin the process of changing your life and becoming more like Him. You will never stop sinning because of your inherent weakness, but when you are born again, you commit yourself to a life of striving to be a better human being, the human being God created you to be.

Two things need to be made clear: not everyone who tells God they are ready for change and are ready to accept His grace is saved. Humans have a natural capability of fooling themselves, but God cannot be fooled. Not only can we fool ourselves, but we can also actually lie to ourselves. How many times have you promised yourself something, and it never happened? You didn't really follow through with it; you just weren't fully committed to it. Saying it doesn't automatically equate to meaning it and saying it when you don't really mean it does not change who you are. Being fully committed, truly believing in your heart what you profess with your lips, is exactly what being born-again means. A profession of faith that you really mean is salvation and the assurance of one day entering the kingdom.

A little side note: when I was first learning about salvation and kept hearing the term 'born-again,' I hated it. I don't quite know why; maybe just because it was a term that was very foreign to me. Being raised Catholic, it was not a term I really had ever heard, and when I first heard it, I didn't like it. To me, it was just one of those weird terms that non-Catholics used. Now that I fully understand its meaning, I could not be any happier to be able to say I am a born-again Christian.

In the New Testament, 2 Peter chapter 2, Peter talks about those 'believers' who are washed on the outside, appearing to be saved, while never changing on the inside. These people are clearly not saved and will eventually revert to their true nature. Peter calls these 'professors' rather than 'possessors' because they profess a changed nature, but it never really happened, and eventually, they drift back to their old nature.

Salvation is a gift. You cannot earn it, you cannot purchase it, you cannot ever do enough to make up for your sins. Some churches believe not only in your ability to achieve salvation through your own efforts but teach that you must earn your way. The Bible is clear; this is not the case. Salvation is strictly a gift, and as such, we can never boast about acquiring it. In a later chapter, I will address good works in more detail and how they may fit into the life of a Christian.

If salvation is the act of removing punishment due as a result of sin, then you also need to know what sin is. Sin is simply doing anything that separates you from God. Simply put, disobedience to God is sin.

God created us to spend eternity with Him, and although He gave us the ability to sin, it was clearly not His desire that we would choose sin over Him. Even after we had sinned, He still wanted us to be able to spend eternity with Him. God had a plan for our salvation. Someone had to pay the price, and only a perfect sacrifice could wipe away the sins of all mankind, sins accumulated from the beginning of creation till the very end. God's plan was allowing His Son to take on human flesh, become man, suffer, and die so that we might live.

It may be difficult to understand why God chose to pay our tab. The simple answer is love. I can only suggest, for lack of a better explanation, that God felt sorry for us, having given us free will, knowing that as much as He loved us, we would still screw up and make some bad choices in life. I think His great love for us would not allow Him to leave us without a lifeboat. He loved us in our sin and chose to create a path for total forgiveness. This path would allow us, in spite of our sin, to still be able to spend eternity with Him. Think of Him as the loving parent that He is. There are few parents who, no matter how far their child may stray, that are not willing to do whatever it takes to save them. I know that there are human parents who would die for their children. So in light of that, is the loving sacrifice by the God who created us so unreasonable?

Thinking about the God who created us being willing to pay for our sins still sounds too good to be true, doesn't it? I know we have always heard that if it sounds too good to be true, it probably is. Well, like most rules, there are always exceptions. This is one of the few cases where, though it sounds too good to be true, it actually is true. Jesus Christ took on our sins, the sins of all mankind, took them to the cross, and at the moment of his death, our sins were no more. Not only forgiven but totally wiped from the 'record.' Jesus paid the price with His blood, and the result is, when we accept His gift, God sees us as pure as the moment we were conceived.

Does that mean everyone goes to heaven because the price was paid? Does it also mean that we can sin all we want because Jesus paid our tab? His death does not give us a free pass to sin. There is one simple yet critical condition, we need to accept the gift and be born-again.

Jesus spent approximately 33 years on the earth and only about three years in His public ministry, during which He told us exactly what we had to do to get this free, prepaid salvation. He said, "Believe in me, accept that I am the Son of God, believe that I died for your sins, repent and be born again." Not too tough, is it? Jesus is saying, "change your life, become a new person, and come follow me." There is nowhere in His teaching where He ever says that we have a price to pay. The bible documents many occasions where after Jesus healed someone, He merely told them to go and sin no more and that their faith had saved them. The key word here is faith. Jesus never said to the prostitute, "go and sin no more, but... you will have to pay a price to be forgiven and to be saved." He told her to change her life, be born-again, period.

Becoming a believer does not mean that life as you know it is over, at least not in the way that you might think. It does not mean you can no longer enjoy life, can't have a beer, smoke a cigarette, dance, go to movies, and so many more fun things. You can certainly find churches and some denomination of Christians who may teach that you can't do a lot of these things. There are groups like the Amish who choose to essentially live in the 19th century, without electricity and many of our everyday conveniences. There is nothing wrong with that way of life, but clearly, the Bible does not suggest that to follow Jesus means we need to forgo all or any of these things.

The Bible is filled with God's promises, and I will tell you this, becoming a Christian does not mean giving up living; it doesn't mean a life of denial and a joyless life. This could not be any further from the truth. There is a true joy that comes from the satisfaction of having Jesus welcome you into His family, and it is a choice that will give you blessings beyond your wildest imagination.

There may be things you won't do anymore, but not because you can't. Your life will change as you choose to be more like Jesus, but not because you 'have to.' I remember something that I was told many years ago regarding going to church; I was told, you 'had' to go to church until you 'wanted' to go to church. Sure, as a Christian, you may find yourself pushing yourself to do things, not because you want to, but because you feel it is the right thing to do. You will find yourself doing things because you want to just because it is a part of the natural changes in your life as you draw nearer to Jesus. Your life is gradually changed from where you thought you wanted to be, to where Jesus wants you to be, and you will find that it is also exactly where you want to be as well.

Following Jesus helps you to become a better *you*, the *you* He created you to be. But He would never force you to become who He wants you to be. However, He will allow you to become that person when you are ready to change.

Remember choices are always yours to make, God will never force you to love Him, He will never force you to follow Him, and He will never force you to live a life you don't choose for yourself. I have always said that we have a gracious God, a God who allows us to make all kinds of mistakes, yet He still loves us.

CHAPTER 6

Will Good People Go to Hell?

No one wants to hear that good people can go to hell. The fact is, many 'good people' will go to hell. I know you are probably saying, *OK, that's it, I'm sure not going accept this Jesus, this loving, just God, who sends good people to hell.* First of all, let's make this point very clear. God sends no one to hell, but He will certainly allow anyone, good or bad, to make that choice. Remember—I can't say it often enough—it is all about choice, which means it is up to you, not God. No one will go to hell because they are good, but it does mean a 'good' person can refuse to accept Jesus and will ultimately pay the price for that choice.

In the Gospel of John, chapter 6, in verse 53, Jesus said, "unless you eat of my flesh and drink my blood, you will have no life in you." And in verse 56, he said, "whoever eats my flesh and drinks my blood remains in me and I in them." This was not taken well by many of His followers and many chose to leave Him because they took His words literally. Jesus was clearly not speaking literally. Jesus taught that He was the bread of life and feeding on Him meant essentially to absorb Him by following Him, by feeding on the Word of God. But many followers said, "this is a hard teaching; who can accept this?"

I bring this up, although it has nothing to do with good people going to hell, but I chose to quote it because I know that this, too, may be a hard teaching to accept. God is not about making you feel comfortable or justifying your thoughts and beliefs. God is more interested in building your character and helping you to become more like Jesus than He is about making you comfortable.

A lot of very good people will go to hell. I know this goes against what you may have heard or what you may want to believe because the world wants you to believe that if you are good or maybe just not bad, you will go to heaven. After all, what kind of loving God would allow 'good people' to go to hell?

We have heard from Jesus' own lips, "For God did not send His Son into the world to condemn the world, but to save the world through Him" (John 3:17 NIV), but eventually, we will all be judged. People like to quote that portion of the text but fail to quote the rest. The very next verse says, "whoever believes in Him is not condemned, but whoever does not believe stands condemned already because he has not believed in the Name of God's one and only Son" (John 3:18 NIV). Although He died to save all mankind, only those who accept His gift shall receive it. You can't reject a gift yet expect to reap the benefits from it. At creation, He endowed us with a free will, the ability to choose Him or to reject Him. He died to save everyone, not a chosen few, but the sad reality may very well be that it is indeed, very few. It has been said, "you will be surprised as to who will be in heaven and equally surprised by who is not." You can't expect to gain heaven or at least avoid hell if you have no idea what is required to get to heaven.

It is sad that in the 21st century, some have watered-down Jesus' teaching so no one will be offended and to make His teaching more 'acceptable.' We don't want to tell anyone that what the world wants us to believe is ok is often simply not ok. We are living in a time when we can't offend anyone. We are living in a period of political correctness gone amok, and it has crept into some churches. There are churches more concerned with filling seats than teaching truth, teaching the Word of God. No one has to excel in anything or accomplish anything to get a trophy. So, it stands to reason, we sure wouldn't want to suggest that Jesus' teachings may mean that some very good people might go to hell. We seem to think we can live under the pretense that we can make up our own rules and code of conduct, ignore what the Bible teaches, and we won't be judged or punished, because after all, God loves us!

Many of us have had the good fortune to have parents who loved us, and yet they disciplined us when we did wrong. We live in a society that punishes people who break laws, at least most of the time, and we consider that justice. Yet, for some reason, we don't think it is justice if God disciplines us. Not disciplining us wouldn't be justice; it would clearly be an injustice. We would scream 'foul' if our courts failed to punish the guilty; so, why do we think God should ignore our guilt? Since God loved us so much that He sent His Son to die for our sins, is it ok to reject Him and assume we can ignore His rules, yet still get a reward?

There is no place in scripture that says good people will or can go to hell. But it is crystal clear that the path to heaven is not about being good; it is about accepting Jesus Christ as one's personal savior. There is one path to heaven, period! You can be a good person, and you can do all kinds of good things; yet, if you refuse to accept Jesus Christ as Lord and Savior, you will not go to heaven. It is just that simple!

The world wants you to believe this could not possibly be true because you are taught that Jesus is all-merciful, all-loving and just, so He couldn't possibly send good people to hell. Although you may not always think about it, there is, at least in the back of your mind somewhere, a punishment you think would be appropriate for a lot of offenses. What should be the punishment for stealing a can of soup? What should be the punishment for physical spousal abuse? What is the right punishment for murder? I know most people feel the punishment should fit the crime. Punishment should be a measured response to be just. What is the measured response for rejecting the love and mercy of our very own creator? What is the appropriate response for turning your back on a God who loved you so much that He allowed Himself to be brutalized by mankind then nailed to a cross and hung up to die a horrible death? Is spending eternity separated from Him not an appropriate, measured response? If not, what is? For just a moment, put yourself in God's shoes, then you decide; what is the appropriate discipline? Should everyone just get a 'participation' trophy?

Justice is about fair consequences. Judges who let everyone coming before them off the hook with a slap on the wrist are not administering justice. Salvation is a case where the reward is great, and so is the punishment; there is no in-between. We are either all-in, or we are out. There is no such thing as being a little preg-nant and there is no such thing as 'kind of' accepting Jesus Christ as your Lord and Savior. You cannot be on the fence about this.

When I think about doing good or just being good to be saved, I like to use the example of Mother Teresa. She spent her entire life doing good, ministering to the poorest of the poor in Calcutta, India. She did not do it to be saved; she did not do it instead of accepting Jesus; she did it because she had accepted Him. She had accepted Jesus Christ as her Lord and Savior, repented of her sins, became a born-again Christian, and became a new person in Christ. Jesus called this new person to serve Him by serving the poor. However, if she had just served the poor her entire life but had never accepted Jesus Christ, she would not have gone to heaven. We do good because of our relationship with Christ, not to gain access to heaven.

I know that it doesn't seem right that someone like Mother Teresa could have gone to hell, no matter how much good she did, if she had not accepted Jesus Christ. Yet, a convicted criminal sentenced to death on a cross could go to heaven. The criminal hanging next to Jesus recognized Him as the Son of God, thereby repenting as he asked Jesus to remember him when he joined His Father in Heaven. There can be no question that his faith in Jesus Christ saved him and certainly not his good works. He may never have done a good thing in his life, but at the end, he reached out to the Son of God and rebuked the other criminal for mocking Jesus. Here is the perfect example of someone who probably never did a good thing in his life, but in his last moments of life, he recognized Jesus for who He was and received salvation, and not a moment too soon. None of us can assume that we can live a life like that criminal, and somehow, we will be given enough time to repent before we take our last breath. The time we have to repent is now, no one has any assurances of a tomorrow.

We cannot work our way into heaven, no matter how good we are and no matter how much good we may do. Jesus made it clear; if we could 'earn' our way, we might be tempted to boast. Since it is purely a gift, none of us can boast of the achievement. If we could ever do enough to make up for our own sins, Jesus' death on the cross would be for nothing.

I would rather live my life believing in God, die, and find out that there is no god than to live my life not believing that God exists and then find out that He does and be doomed for eternity because I failed to acknowledge Him. Believing has only an upside; there is no downside. You certainly will not be punished for believing in God if it turns out there is none, but God promised that there are consequences for not believing. Are you willing to gamble on eternity?

Sometimes I feel like the apostle Peter; knowing what I know, I cannot remain silent. If I failed to share my most precious possession, my faith in Jesus Christ, it would be like being the world's richest man and not be willing to share my wealth and be willing to sit back and watch people around me starve. There are essentially people all around me 'starving,' people who have not accepted Jesus Christ and will not make it to heaven. If I can save one of you from 'starvation,' I will have lived a life worth living.

In today's world, many would like to believe that hell doesn't really exist. Wouldn't it be great if no matter what choices you make in life, there would never be consequences for bad decisions and choices? The world wants you to believe that fallacy and accept that you can live life any way you choose; you are in charge of your own destiny and there are no end-of-life consequences. Well, they are partially true; you are absolutely in charge of your own destiny; you can choose to live life any way you want. However, the truth is this: there are consequences for making the wrong choices.

Jesus was the man God intended each of us to be.

CHAPTER 7
How to Study the Bible

The title of this Chapter may sound like I am implying that there is a right way and a wrong way to study the Word of God, but there is not. It is far more important that you make a commitment to study than making any decision as to how to study.

If you are ready to start the process toward knowing God and developing a relationship with Jesus Christ, then the time to start is now. How should you choose a version of the Bible to study? That there are multiple 'versions' of the Bible does not mean these Bibles differ in content. The various versions refer to the different translations of the original Greek, Hebrew, and Aramaic texts. This may sound as though the end result can be different, and unfortunately, to some degree, that is accurate. However, let me clarify a little further. Some methods may give the most accurate translation and others may make for an easier read. You may be familiar with the very early English translations with all the 'thees' and 'thous' that tend to make reading the Bible very difficult, as no one speaks that kind of English today. Then there are very 'loose' translations that make easy reading the priority. I have to admit that some of these 'loose' translations do make reading easier, but at the same time, I fear that sometimes they so 'loosely' translate a word or phrase for the sake of the easy read that the meaning sometimes is lost.

If you accept that God wrote, or more accurately, inspired the Bible, it is of utmost importance that you find a Bible version that you are confident does not deviate from what He inspired the authors to write. That certainly would defeat its purpose. It would be a little like a doctor telling you that he has good news and bad news for you. The good news is that you have a year to live; the bad news is that I should have told you this 11 months ago. In this case, it is just about timing, but when it comes to the Bible, it is about eternity, and getting it right is critical. You certainly do not want a Bible that is easy to read yet loses a critical part of God's message; your eternal life is at stake.

In the earliest of times, before printing presses when Bibles had to be handwritten, there had to be great care taken to assure that every word was copied correctly. These early scribes, those who hand wrote the Bibles, were often referred to as counters because they counted every word and every letter as an assurance that they were copying it correctly and nothing was missed or lost in the copy process.

When it comes to versions, my personal favorite is the NIV, the New International Version. It is fairly easy to read, but I selected it because I studied the process that they used to create the NIV. There are versions out there that merely take a current version such as the King James version or one of many other versions and just update the language to make it easier to read. When that type of translation is done, it is like making a copy of a copy of a copy of a photo. Over time, each subsequent copy loses a little of the resolution, and after enough copies, you no longer get all the detail that was in the original photo. This would be similar to the experiment where a message is verbally passed along a row of people and by the time it gets to the last person, even if the last person in the row understands it, it may very well bear no resemblance to the original message given the first person. There are two major considerations in making a choice of versions: ease of reading as well as retention of the meaning of God's inspired word.

There are various ways that the Bible has been translated. One of those is the word for word, or strict literal translation, where each individual word is translated. Then there is phrase-to-phrase or thought-for-thought translation. In the thought-for-thought translation, the translators are attempting to convey clearly the thought in that phrase rather than literally translating each individual word. The word-for-word translation is considered to be a very literal translation, and this can tend to make reading a little awkward, yet less likely to lose meaning. A literal translation from the ancient Greek text to English does not allow for a smooth flow of thought since there are significantly different grammatical rules for Greek and English. You should be very leery of paraphrase translations. These will be easy reads but often are the translation of a single person who reads the Bible, then rewrites it into their version of what they believe the phrase or paragraph is saying without a real understanding of the meaning of the Greek or Aramaic words that it was translated from. The paraphrase method is really the most like the previous example of a copy of a copy. If I were to read a verse in the Bible and without understanding the specific meaning of the Greek or Aramaic words that it was translated from, yet rewrote the verse to say what I thought the verse was conveying, there is a high probability that I could lose what God intended that verse to say. Remember, the Bible is not a novel; maintaining accuracy is crucial.

I tend to lean more toward a phrase-to-phrase, also known as a thought-for-thought translation, which has put great effort into conveying the original meaning of the Greek text. When you select a version of the Bible to study, remember that your salvation depends on obeying the Word of God, so you will definitely want a version that is both accurate and understandable.

The NIV version is a completely new translation of the Bible and was the work of over a hundred scholars. This version, completed in the 1970s, was not a rewrite of other versions but was translated directly from the earliest available Hebrew, Aramaic, and Greek texts. It is considered to be a phrase-for-phrase translation and is a relatively easy version to read. The group that developed the version was not made up of any 'official' church representatives, but was a trans-denominational group; yet, its conclusions were endorsed by many leaders from many denominations. Once again, it is my favorite, but when you choose one, do your own research. Know how the version was translated and from which documents. You can also go online and read a little from various versions to help you pick the one you would like to use for your study.

The Bible is the ONLY way that you can get to know God, and

He does want you to know Him. The goal is not only to know Him but to have an up-close personal relationship with Him. The most basic Christian teachings that children learn from the earliest age is this: God created us to know Him, love Him and serve Him. The first part of that is KNOW Him. He wants you to know Him, not just know *about* Him. There are many ways you can know about Him but the only way you can really know Him is to study Him through a study of His Word.

There is no right way or wrong way to study His Word. My method for study is this: I read a chapter, the same chapter every day, along with a supplemental study guide for an entire week. There are many study guides, but I prefer one that helps set the stage, which helps with a better understanding by giving the background of what may have been going on at the time the chapter was written. This helps to add clarity to what the writer is saying. Sometimes, it is a historical background; sometimes, it is a better definition of the words used or a notation that the word used in one instance is the same word used in another text that helps to better understand the context of the word. An example that I have used is the English word *love*. In this particular case, the writer used the Greek word *agape*, which translates to *love* but is a special kind of love. *Agape love* is the kind of love that God has for us. It is unearned and quite possibly undeserved. It is not linked to anything that we may have done. It is unconditional love; God loves us just *because*.

I use *Wiersbe's Expository Outlines*[9, 10] as my study guide. For me, my study method works, and I find that by the time I get to the end of the week, I feel I have acquired a pretty good understanding of the message of the chapter. Granted, this takes a very long time to get through the entire Bible, but then, it's not a race.

How you study is definitely your choice, but if you are picking up a Bible for the first time, I think that reading the four Gospels chronicling the life of Jesus would be a good start. Although John happens to be the last of the four, I suggest reading it first. Then continue on to the remaining three Gospels and on through the rest of the New Testament. I suggested the Gospel of John first, as I find his Gospel the easiest to read. It does vary from the other three Gospels in that the other three are referred to as the synoptic Gospels because there is a lot of overlap of the events they describe. John is different; he does not include any of Jesus' parables and does describe miracles not covered by the other three writers. I find John's Gospel shows a more personal side of Jesus. John was probably closer to Jesus than any of the other apostles, although Peter was considered a leader and was also very close. However, it was John whom Jesus asked to care for His mother as He was dying on the cross. John primarily wrote his Gospel to give evidence of the divinity of Jesus, but at the same time chose to show the very human side of Jesus, a man who occasionally was tired, sad, angry, loving, showing all human emotions. You may consider a one-time read through before attempting an in-depth study. Get to know about Him, then get to know Him.

The rest is up to you and the Holy Spirit, whose job it is to assist you in getting whatever God intended for you to get out of your study. Even though it was written 2000 years ago, it was written *for* you and *to* you. But it takes effort. You can't sleep with the Bible on your nightstand or sit a fancy Bible on your living room bookshelf or coffee table and assume that the Holy Spirit will magically get the message to you through some kind of spiritual osmosis. You have to pick it up, open it, read it and study it.

God is telling you that He left His word especially for you and provided the Holy Spirit to assist you, but you still need to put in the work. He is saying, "come to me, I really want us to know each other." He already knows everything about you, and He would like you to know everything about Him as well. That's how relationships are built.

CHAPTER 8
Are There Rules?

We find in the Apostle Paul's letter to the Colossians, chapter 2, verse 14 (NIV), *"Having canceled the written code, with its regulations, that was against us and that stood opposed to us; He took it away, nailing it to the cross."* We also read in Paul's letter to the Galatians in chapter 3, verse 23-25 (NIV), *"Before faith came, we were held prisoners by the law, locked up until faith should be revealed. So, the law was put in charge to lead us to Christ that we might be justified by faith. Now that faith has come, we are no longer under the supervision of the law."*

I am not suggesting there are no rules, that you can live however you choose to live and all is good. That seems to be the worldly view but clearly not one I am suggesting or what Paul is saying either.

If you have not accepted Jesus Christ as your Lord and Savior, there are indeed rules; all of the commandments definitely apply. What Paul is saying is that once you have been born again into Christ, the rules are no longer pertinent. Paul is saying a follower of Jesus does not need a lot of 'thou shalt nots.' A follower of Jesus chooses to follow the example set by Jesus and no longer needs rules to guide them. He is saying that faith in Jesus is what frees us from the law.

Jesus said that He did not come to do away with the law but to fulfill it. Many take this comment to mean that the law, Mosaic Law, and all the commandments are still very much intact. I am telling you these rules, these laws, no longer bind believers. I know you have to be asking yourself, how can this be so, how can we not have laws to follow? First of all, no one has ever been saved by the law, the Mosaic law, the Ten Commandments or any other laws. We are never saved by laws but are saved by the blood of Jesus, shed on the cross.

Jesus came to change that whole concept. He was a *do what I do* kind of guy, rather than don't do this or that or else! Jesus preached a relationship with Him, with the Father, a relationship not based on fear or following rules. Jesus said, "I came to fulfill the law." Fulfilling the law means a transition from obeying laws to following Jesus and choosing to live a godly life. God always intended man to live the life that Jesus Himself lived, a life that needs no laws but one that is the personification of the law.

You might say, so what is the difference? Living a godly life or obeying laws—they seem to be the same thing. The end result is the same thing, a sinless life, but a life based on the desire to do good rather than obeying laws to keep oneself from doing bad things; that is the difference. The result is the same; it's the process that is different. When you choose to follow Jesus, you are freely choosing to change your life and not out of fear of the consequences. The difference is choice.

I once read this, and I can't give proper credit because I can't recall where I read it, but it went something like this: most states have laws that require parents to care for their children or they can end up in jail. Do most parents care for their children out of fear of going to jail? No, certainly not. Most parents care for their children out of their love for them. That is precisely the kind of relationship God wants with us. He wants us to love Him because we choose to, not out of any fear of pending consequences if we do not.

Jesus challenges us to live a life that needs no laws. It's not an easy concept to tell someone that they don't have to obey any laws, but the fact is that if we live a life in the shadow of Jesus, there is no need to worry about laws. For example: if I were to ask you to drive across Michigan's Mackinac Bridge without any guard rails to keep you from falling off the edge of this five-mile-long bridge, it certainly would seem terrifying. Consider the guard rails as the law that keeps you on the straight and narrow and keeps you from falling over the edge. If you drive a path that follows Jesus, staying within the lines, right down the center of your lane, there is no need to have guard rails to keep you in, because you are driving a path going nowhere near the edge or close to the guardrails. You wouldn't drive across the bridge scraping along the guard rails, so the only thing preventing you from going over the edge is the guardrails. You would choose to drive in your lane, nowhere near the guard rails, so the question is: do you really need them? Jesus is saying to you, follow me and you will have no need for laws. Laws are meant for the lawless, and followers of Jesus are not lawless. Laws were intended to bring people to God, once you come to Him, you no longer need them.

I imagine that you are more comfortable with rules, a safety net, guardrails on the highway of life, but God is telling you that laws are not for His people. It can be equated to locks on your doors. You don't lock your doors at night, or any time for that matter, to keep out the good and honest people. They respect your property and your privacy. Locks are intended for the untrustworthy, the would-be thieves. In the same way, God is telling you the rules that existed before Jesus' death on the cross are for the unsaved; they do not apply to His people, the believers.

So, does this mean there are no laws? No, it does not. What it does mean is that believers are expected to obey the laws Jesus gave us, namely, love one another as I have loved you, love the Lord your God with your whole heart and your whole being, and come follow me. Follow me does not mean, 'kind of' follow me, and 'kind of' try to live the life that I lived. Jesus calls you to be born-again, to be willing to change who you are and become ready to be more like Him. Jesus commanded us to do things; He didn't give us commands about what we shall not do. His life was all about example and about love. He asked us to love God, to love each other, to care for the poor, to be compassionate, and the list goes on. Once again, all about being like Him.

God doesn't want you to draw near to Him out of fear of breaking the rules. He wants you to draw near to Him because you have learned to love Him just like He loves you. Jesus once said, *"if you love me, you will obey my com-*

mands." He linked obedience to love, not fear. We tend to think of the word 'obey' in negative terms, something we do out of fear of retribution, but the 'obey' that Jesus wants is obedience grown out of love.

CHAPTER 9
Explaining the Unexplainable

Explaining the unexplainable is somewhat of an oxymoron as well as risky business for me to think I might have the ability to explain the unexplainable. It would also be very foolhardy. I certainly may not be able to explain these things, but I will attempt to, at least, put some of these unexplainable things into some kind of perspective that might help a little with understanding them. I do accept that there may be aspects of Christianity that some call mysteries. Whether we term them as unexplainable or mysteries is not really important, but we have to accept that there will always be things about God that are beyond our ability, as mere human beings, to comprehend.

You can choose to look at things in the Bible that you don't understand in a couple of ways; either God does not want or need you to know or understand every aspect about Him, or He just wants you to trust Him enough to accept that it is so, purely because He said it was. End of story.

You can have total confidence that anything you need to know to be saved will not be vague or difficult to understand. The Bible contains many absolutes that leave no room for misunderstanding. Some issues are far less clear and God will reveal them to you when and if He needs you to know them.

An example of a non-absolute is the issue of baptism. Some churches believe you must be baptized to be saved, and if you die without being baptized, you cannot go to heaven. Biblically, there is no truth to that assertion. There is no doubt that Jesus did indeed command us to be baptized, but it has nothing to do with salvation. If we examine the issue of baptism, we find that Jesus said that to be saved, we must be born-again. Being born-again is the all-inclusive requirement to be saved. Being born-again is the internal decision to accept Jesus Christ as Lord and Savior, repent and change one's life. Now granted, Jesus did command us to be baptized, but this was to be done as an outward sign of what had already happened on the inside, literally being reborn. Baptism is purely a symbolic act to openly show that we have been reborn. We are baptized out of obedience to Jesus' wishes, not to be saved.

The second issue regarding baptism is that there are churches who baptize by pouring water over the forehead, and there are those who insist that one must be fully immersed. It seems clear that Jesus, as well as all early converts to Christianity, were immersed, but does it really matter? The answer has to be no. If the method of baptism was in any way essential to us being obedient to His command, be assured that the Bible would not be ambiguous about how it should be done. It is merely a public declaration of our salvation. A changed heart is what saves us, not water, whether immersed in it or having it poured over our forehead.

Another 'mystery,' or at least a reasonable question is, did Jesus always exist, or did God create Him? Jesus is the Son of God and a person within our singular God, He was not created. John starts his gospel with the following, *"In the beginning was the Word, and the Word was with God, and the Word was God. He was with God in the beginning. Through Him all things were made; without Him nothing was made that has been made"* (John 1:1-3 NIV). John refers to Jesus as the Word, and he makes that fact clear in the following when he said, *"The Word became flesh and made His dwelling among us"* (John 1:14a NIV). Had John been writing his gospel in 21st century American English, he probably would have said, "In the beginning was Jesus, and Jesus was with God and Jesus was God. Jesus created everything, and there is nothing that exists that He did not create." This is clearly an example of a paraphrase translation.

John is saying that Jesus is indeed God and that as God He is and always was God. As God, He is also the Creator, and this person, a part of the Triune God (God existing in three persons), is the person of God that became flesh and lived among us.

The Bible tells us that our single God is also God the Father, God the Son, and God the Holy Spirit, so there is no doubt that there are three distinct persons in this single God.

The Book of Matthew, chapter 28, verse 19, quotes Jesus, who said, *"Go ye therefore, and teach all nations, baptizing them in the name of the Father, and of the Son, and of the Holy Spirit."* This and other references in the Bible clearly address the three persons, or the less popular belief, three personalities.

I guess this is clearly one of those things one can consider a mystery since we can't quite comprehend three persons in a single God. For me, there is a fine line distinction between mystery and mysterious. I don't like to think of God and Christianity as mysterious, but there certainly are things that we cannot comprehend.

I know that the following example will not fully explain the Trinity, three persons in this single God, but let's use ourselves as an example. We are each a multiple of 'persons,' but for the sake of this discussion, let's consider each of us as being three persons. I can be a father, a husband, and a breadwinner (worker), yet I am still one; a woman can be at least three things as well: mother, wife, and breadwinner, too. I also know that most women would tell you they wish they only had to be three different people to do what they have to do as a wife and mother. In these cases, they are the same single human being yet functioning at various times as different persons fulfilling distinctly different roles. I know that the Trinity of God is not the same, but this example may help you to comprehend the concept just a little better.

Some Christian scholars differ when defining the 'three persons,' as some will clearly say that they are distinct 'persons' while others claim that they are not persons, but 'personalities' of one person, one God. We may be splitting hairs here, and I know that how we choose to deal mentally with this 'mystery' is irrelevant. Why? Because we don't have to know how to sort out these things to be saved. The opinion held by most scholars is that the Trinity is composed of three very distinct persons and not personalities.

There will always be those who try to poke holes in anything relating to God or religion. "If you can't understand it, it can't be real" is not a very sound argument. One simple analogy is a clover. It has three distinct leaves, but it is still one single clover. Sure, a little oversimplification, maybe, but think about this. Would we not expect the creator of all things, to be just a little more complex than His creation? And let's face it, His creation is pretty darn complex. Finding things about our Creator that are just a little too complex for us to grasp is not to be unexpected.

You will surely discover that there are things in the Bible that are not really clear to you, but not to worry; if it were important enough that God wanted you or expected you to fully understand, He would have made it abundantly clear. There are always going to be things that God just simply wants you to accept on faith just because you believe and trust Him and have no reason to question it. Most of us have someone in our life that we fully trust, and when they tell us something, we simply know that we do not have to question it. We simply believe because there is no reason to assume this trusted person is telling us something that is not true. God wants you to accept some of these things in that same way, by just having enough trust in Him that you know, if He says it, it is simply so, period, end of discussion.

I'm going to touch on something that may make theologians cringe. I have never heard a Biblical scholar or theologian ever discuss this subject. Even though Jesus Christ was fully God and fully man, as I read scripture, it becomes clear to me that there are at least some definite lines drawn between God's Son and the fully human Jesus Christ. In the Gospel of John, we read, *"Jesus gave them this answer, 'I tell you the truth, the Son can do nothing by Himself; He can do only what He sees His Father doing'"* (John 5:19a NIV). The Gospel of Mark says, *"But about that day or hour no one knows, not even the angels in heaven, nor the Son, but only the Father"* (Mark 13:32 NIV). There are several occasions in the Bible where Jesus speaks of things that the Son is not privy to. I can only accept that in these occasions, He is speaking of the human Son, since the Son of God would have all knowledge, being a part of the person of God.

Another example of the separation, or at least what certainly appears to be a separation, between Jesus Christ the Son of God and Jesus Christ the man, is when Jesus was near death on the cross,

He called out, *"my God, my God why have you forsaken me?"* At that very moment, Jesus was fulfilling the very reason He became man. As He took on all of mankind's sins for that brief moment in time as He drew His last breath, He was separated from the Father. Separation from God is the definition of sin. At the moment of His death, He was again reunited with the Father as all that sin had now been wiped away. He had just paid the price in full.

That Jesus also often spoke of He and the Father being one also makes it clear that Jesus, the Son of God, is clearly at one with the Father. In the Gospel of John, the apostle Philip said, "Lord, show us the Father and that will be enough for us." Jesus answered, *"Don't you know me, Philip, even after I have been among you such a long time? Anyone who has seen me has seen the Father. How can you say, 'Show us the Father?'"*

These are only a few examples found in the Gospels, often from the very words of Jesus Himself, that lead me to believe that although God the Son and the Father are one as well as the Holy Spirit, there is still some degree of separation between Jesus the human being and Jesus the Son of God. There will always be these kinds of things that will just have to be accepted as facts, based on trust and faith. There will always be things beyond the comprehension of the human mind. As humans, our understanding of things is generally based on a frame of reference. We have no frame of reference here.

Can we explain the color blue to a person who was born blind and had never seen anything ever? It would be difficult at best but probably impossible because there is no frame of reference. To someone who may not have always been blind and had seen colors, we may be able to describe a new shade of a color, because there is a frame of reference. With God, the entire concept forces us to deal with something that we cannot put into any frame of reference. We know no one else who can create something out of nothing, who has always been and always will be and has no beginning and no end. For some, refusing to accept the existence of God is easier than trying to accept something that cannot be fully understood. It certainly would be arrogant, at the very least, to say that if you cannot comprehend it and if you cannot prove it, therefore it does not exist. It would be like denying the existence of electricity or the internet, merely because you can't fully explain it. Most of us know what it can do, but how many of us can really explain electricity or the internet? But we sure know they exist.

Here are just a couple of references from the Gospel of John, quoting Jesus:

- *"If you love me, keep my commandments. I will ask the Father to give you another Helper, to be with you always. He is the Spirit of truth, whom the world cannot receive, because it neither sees Him nor recognizes Him. But you recognize Him, because He lives with you and will be in you"* (John 14:15-17 NIV).

- *"But the Helper, the Holy Spirit, whom the Father will send in my name, will teach you all things and remind you of everything that I have told you"* (John 14:26 NIV).

Scripture does not give us a clear picture of the Holy Spirit, but more often, the references to the Spirit are about His function or mission rather than a description of Him.

CHAPTER 10

What's Love Got To Do with It?

The title of this chapter just happens to be the title of a Tina Turner song as well as the title of a 1993 movie about her life with Ike Turner. Trust me, there wasn't a lot of love going on there.

With God, love has everything to do with it. I mentioned earlier that the Greek language, in which many of the earliest known documents that would become the New Testament were written, had multiple words for *love,* while in English, we have only one. The love that God has for us is the Greek word *agape.* The associate pastor who performed our marriage called it a 'just because' kind of love. He said that God loved us 'just because' and not because we were or did anything special. It is a love that clearly is not merited or earned; in fact, it is the exact opposite. God loves us so much that even when we were sinners, He chose to freely give His life on a cross, shedding every drop of His blood so that our sins would be forgiven. That is agape love, and that is giving your all. And it should be the same kind of love that a husband and wife share, who love each other 'just because.' A couple may fall in love for a multitude of reasons, but to stay in love, they have to be able to look beyond all of their little faults and continue to love each other 'just because.'

Wiersbe, in his Expository Outlines, said, "God's love flows from us as we yield to the Spirit. Christians do not love each other because of their good qualities, but in spite of their bad qualities." That is exactly the love that God has for each of us. He surely does not love most of us because of our good qualities but in spite of our bad qualities. That is God's unconditional, unearned, agape love.

I have often said when referring to my children that some of their good qualities came from me, and others were in spite of me. But no matter what qualities they may have, my love for them can never change. I do consider myself really blessed because they turned out with so many good qualities, and fortunately for us, our God looks at us in that very same way. His love for us is never based on our qualities, but just the same, I can imagine that He is very pleased when it turns out that we have acquired some good ones.

You can give without loving, but you cannot love without giving. If you love without giving, believe me, it isn't love. For this is love, not that we loved, but that He loved us first and gave His Son to save us from our sins.

The Gospel of John tells us that God so loved the world that He gave His one and only Son so that whosoever believed in Him would have eternal life. Can you even begin to understand what it means for Him to give His Son to die for someone else's transgressions? It would be like sending your son to prison to serve a sentence for a criminal so that criminal could go free. Hard to imagine anyone willing to do that, but that is exactly what God did for us 'criminals.' We deserved punishment, but Jesus paid the price so we would not have to.

The apostle John said, *"Dear friends, let us love one another, for love comes from God. Everyone who loves has been born of God and knows God. Whoever does not love does not know God, because God is love. This is how God showed His love among us: He sent His one and only Son into the world that we might live through Him. This is love: not that we loved God, but that he loved us and sent His Son as an atoning sacrifice for our sins. Dear friends, since God so loved us, we also ought to love one another. No one has ever seen God; but if we love one another, God lives in us and His love is made complete in us"* (1 John 4:7-12 NIV).

The essence of our God is love, and that love is manifested in His gifts to us. Everything that we have is a gift from Him—the air we breathe, the planet we live on, the fact that our heart is beating and pumping blood throughout our bodies—these are all gifts from God. We like to take credit for the 'things' that we have accumulated or accomplished—our jobs, our homes, our cars and on and on and on. We need to take a step back and ask ourselves who provided us the very talents that allowed us to accumulate all of this? Who provided our health or the abilities that allowed us to make a living or accumulate wealth?

A long time ago, I was sharing with a friend that I was grateful to God for what I had in my life, and he argued that God didn't give me these things; I earned them. There certainly is some truth to that, but as I said in the last paragraph, that ability to come as far as I have was due to God, who provided all things. Every night, before I present God with my long list of prayer requests, I thank Him first for such things as the good parents I was born to, the great country I was born into, the time in history when I was born, and the awesome wife and children that God blessed me with. There can be no question that these are all things that I had absolutely no control over.

I said that the essence of God is love manifested in His giving. The Bible mentions giving more times than heaven and hell combined, so it would seem that giving is important to God.

CHAPTER 11
What is Faith?

Can you imagine a world where you could not depend on or count on anyone or anything? Most of us put trust in someone or something. You may put money in a bank, trusting that the bank will be able to give you your money whenever you choose to ask for it. You climb a ladder, trusting that it will hold you up and you will not fall. You enter an elevator, trusting that it will take you to the floor you select. There are countless things that you place trust in every day, and you may not refer to it as faith, but that is what it is.

Can you make it through your entire life without ever having faith in God and His Son, Jesus Christ? You and I both know very well that the answer is, of course, you can. But the real question is, what about the next life? If you have absolute assurance that there is no life after this one, then you are still exhibiting faith, a faith that you are right. I am asking you to take a good hard look and think about all the things you have read so far. Are you still so positive that faith in Jesus Christ is not necessary? If there is even the slightest possibility that there is a hereafter and faith in Jesus Christ is the only way to assure an eternity free from punishment, you just might want to consider trusting in Him.

I have really thought about this topic a lot, and it is not easy to explain. I said in the preface that I didn't want this book to be about me. However, I thought and thought about this chapter and found it hard to explain faith without talking about my own. At least let me explain why I believe so strongly. There are not a lot of things in this world that we can be sure about; we have all heard that the only two things that we can be sure about are death and taxes. I'd like to think that there are more.

There was a period in my life when I may not have actually stopped believing in God; I guess He was still there, but I had strayed so far from faith that it rarely, if ever, crossed my consciousness. You may be in that same place. You may never have had faith, never believed, or, like me, put it so far back in your consciousness that you don't ever give it a thought.

At one point, my life had pretty much spiraled out of control, I knew that my family, especially my own children, had become embarrassed by me and the life that I was living, yet I felt helpless to do anything about it. I do know one thing for certain; I did not like the person that I had become. Then something unexplainable started to happen in my life, events started falling into place that caused my life to change, and the only rational explanation for me was God at work in my life. It had reached a point where I could no longer ignore that an external force was at work. As much as I may have wanted to, I just could not explain away what was happening to me other than the God whom I had chosen to ignore for such a long time clearly had not forgotten or ignored me. I found myself doing things driven by faith, knowing that it was God's plan for me. I found myself so sure that what was happening was God's will that I was truly fearful of not doing what I felt I was being led to do. I was too afraid to ignore it, and I was far less fearful of what I was about to do than what might happen if I choose not to do what I believed God was telling me to do. This was the same God that I totally ignored for years, and now it seemed He was causing things to happen in my life. I believed all of it could only be attributed to Him 'meddling' in my life.

I did something very terrifying. I quit a job, a really good job that I had for 21 years, essentially giving up everything, loaded what I could fit into my car, and moved more than 2,000 miles across the country. The next 2 ½ years was nothing short of life-changing. I loved where I was living and the new life that I had begun to build during those 2 ½ years. But then this God was now telling me to move back across the country for what I believed was going to be a nine-month job that ended up lasting fourteen years.

During those 2 ½ years, I had started praying to the God that I had disregarded for so long. By this time in my life, I had three failed marriages, and I was alone but didn't want to be. I prayed, asking God to bring someone into my life but made it clear that I was leaving it entirely in His hands, as I no longer trusted my own judgment in that area of my life. If it was His will for me to have someone in my life, He was going to have to provide her.

I made the move back across the country, a move that I made kicking and screaming. I didn't want to do it, but in my mind, God was clearly behind this move. Not long after (there is a long story but I'll stick to the short version), I met my wife. I also got to spend precious time with my aging parents until my father died at 95 and most of the years with my mother until she died at 102.

When I headed back across the country that last time, I did believe that it was going to be for only 9 months, and then I would make the cross-country trek once again. Little did I know that it would take fourteen more years for that to happen. So many things happened in my life that I just cannot deny faith in Him and His involvement in my life. How could I deny what was so very obvious? Remember, I asked you to use logic, reasoning, and just plain old common sense rather than preconceived ideas. Common sense was clearly telling me that all the things happening in my life could not be attributed to coincidence. Sure, there are coincidences in life, but then there are those kinds of things that began to happen regularly that I just couldn't continue to brush off as chance. There are coincidences and there are God-incidences.

If you choose to accept most of life as random chance, maybe you need to take another look at nature. Think about Monarch butterflies and the rest of nature, then tell me, *sure it may be kind of unique but it's just random chance, just evolution, no one is really watching over all of it. It just happened that everything works the way it does.* Accepting all that as merely random occurrences takes more faith than believing in a God. Doesn't having faith in a God Creator seem more reasonable than random chance and coincidence?

Merriam-Webster's defines faith as:
- *allegiance to duty or a person: lost faith in the company's*

president
- fidelity to one's promises
- sincerity of intentions acted in good faith
- belief and trust in and loyalty to God
- belief in the traditional doctrines of a religion
- firm belief in something for which there is no proof
- complete trust
- *something that is believed especially with strong conviction especially: a system of religious beliefs*

Faith is accepting something to be true, although we may not be able to prove it beyond any doubt. Our minds are already filled with things we choose to accept on faith. Can most of us prove that the circumference of the earth is 24,901 miles or that sound travels at 2.914 miles in 4.689 seconds? Certainly, some scientists can verify these numbers, but we accept them purely on faith. So often, we read things and, without question, believe them to be true. We are constantly exposed to all kinds of facts; we just accept and don't question, but when it comes to God, all of a sudden, we want proof.

CHAPTER 12
Now What?

As we near the end of the book, I will not dare to assume that you have miraculously become a believer, and you are now ready to accept Jesus Christ as your personal Lord and Savior. Since the whole purpose of the book is that someone might be led to that conclusion, it would certainly be great if that were the case, but I am also realistic. I hope that I have, at the very least, given you something to think about. I would hope that what you have read has brought you to the point of taking the very first step, accepting that what you have read is at least possible and reasonable.

What if nothing you have read here is true? At the same time, you also have to be ready to ask yourself, what if it is? What if every word of this book is absolutely true? Are you willing to gamble on it? Are you going to just walk away at this point, or are you at least willing to accept the possibility? Don't you owe it to yourself to explore further?

If you are just not sure, not quite ready to come to Jesus, ask Him to do what the man in the Gospel of Mark 9:22-24 (NIV) does. A man's son was sick and the man came to Jesus and asked Him, "*If you can do anything, take pity on us and help us.*" "*If you can?*" said Jesus. "*Everything is possible for one who believes.*" Immediately the boy's father exclaimed, "*I do believe; help me overcome my unbelief!*" This is not only a truly beautiful prayer; it is so completely honest. The man was admitting that he believed and certainly hoped that Jesus could help, but there was just that bit of natural skepticism, so he asked Jesus to help him to overcome any doubt. You will have moments of unbelief, moments when you may doubt your God is big enough or willing enough to heal the brokenness in you, but when you ask for help to overcome any unbelief, you can be sure that help is on the way.

Prayers are not always answered the way you would like them to be answered. If they are answered, they may not be answered in the time frame you would like. God will always listen, and He does answer every single request. But God is not a genie. You can't just make wishes and expect you will receive everything you ask for. God will answer in the same manner that any responsible parent might answer their child's wishes. When a child asks for something, the answer may be "no;" sometimes, it may be "not right now;" other times, the answer is a resounding "yes." Some prayers that are always answered in the affirmative are prayers for guidance and prayers for help with your faith or with your unbelief. When you ask for help when you pray, expect God to answer. Be patient and allow God to answer before blindly proceeding. If you don't wait for an answer, aren't you really telling Him that you don't need or expect His help?

When you talk to God, you cannot hear Him with the TV or radio blaring or if you are doing all the talking. Be patient and be quiet; answers will come. The apostle James, the brother of Jesus, said, "when he asks, he must believe and not doubt, because he who doubts is like a wave of the sea, blown and tossed by the wind. That man should not think that he will receive anything from the Lord." James is saying, *if you do not believe He will answer, you can be pretty sure that you will not get one.* The Bible also says that you received not because you asked not.

There is a saying that goes like this: 'if it is big enough to worry about, it is big enough to pray about, and if it is big enough to pray about, you don't need to worry about it.' When you pray, pray with faith, trusting that once you put it into God's hands, you can clear your plate. God's got it.

We need to stop trying to squeeze the God of our understanding into a mold that fits our needs and wishes and start looking to the God that wants us to fit into His mold. Do you really want to create a God that will accept whatever you want to believe is right, but have no real interest in finding out what He declares to be right? Yes, God is loving, He is merciful and just, but that does not mean that you can do, think, and act as you see fit and assume that this loving God will not discipline you.

I recently came across this statement that was attributed to Rick Warren, pastor and author. I agree with it and think it is an appropriate comment to include here:

"Our culture has accepted two huge lies. The first is that if you disagree with someone's lifestyle, you must hate them. The second is to love someone means that you agree with everything they believe or do. Both are nonsense. You don't have to compromise convictions to be compassionate."[11]

In John chapter 3, verses 17 and 18, Jesus said, *"For God did not send his Son into the world to condemn the world, but to save the world through Him. Whoever believes in Him is not condemned, but whoever does not believe stands condemned already because he has not believed in the name of God's only Son."*

If you want to believe, God will give you the ability. God will always provide whatever is necessary for you to achieve anything He calls you to do. Noah had never built an Ark before God asked Him. Peter, Paul, and the other apostles had never started a worldwide movement until Jesus told them to go and preach the Gospel to the entire world. Matthew, Mark, Luke, and John had never written a book until God called them to document the life and teachings of Jesus Christ.

Do not be put off by someone who professes to be a Christian who does not, in any way, exemplify the teachings of the Jesus they profess to follow. It is about your choice to follow Jesus, not about someone else's lack of sincerity in their 'relationship' with Him. Judging others tends to come naturally, but judging others is not in your job description. A relationship with God has to be a one-on-one relationship, and it is only between you and Him. We are all capable of sin, and we are all capable of being hypocrites, but it is not your job to point them out.

Christian should be able to say, "if you have seen me, you have seen Jesus." In reality, this may not be the case, but as Christians, that is clearly what Jesus is expecting of us. We should be a reflection of Jesus. Don't judge Jesus or Christianity by judging the shortcomings of some of His 'followers.' Being born-again does not turn us into perfect humans, but we are expected to continue to be a work in progress.

If I have accomplished nothing more than rousing your curiosity, let me suggest a possible next step. There are a lot of great books that you might find very interesting, but here are a few of my favorites. *The Case for Christ*, by Lee Strobel. Lee is a man who married a believer. However, Lee was such a strong disbeliever that he set out on a mission to prove to his wife that her faith was founded in fantasy rather than fact. He set out to prove beyond any doubt that Jesus was not God and that believing in Him was foolhardy. Instead, the end result of his extensive research to prove her wrong ended up proving to himself that Jesus was exactly who He said He was. If you choose to read his book, you will see exactly how extensive his research was.[12]

Another book that I recommend is *God's Not Dead: Evidence of God in an Age of Uncertainty*, by Rice Broocks,[13] and one final choice, *Stealing from God: Why Atheists Need God to Make Their Case*, by Frank Turek.[14] There are so many excellent books that just might help you move forward in faith if that is a choice you'd like to make.

Also, if you are ready to continue the journey, find a church. I cannot stress enough the importance of doing that. Jesus established the church for a reason. Man does not live in a vacuum, and it is important for believers, and even those who are merely exploring, to connect with others who are in the same position, either searching or growing in faith. God wants us to come together. He wants us to share with like-minded people, and He wants us to worship together. The right church is also important; don't give up if the first church you try doesn't seem to be a fit. The right church for you is out there, and you will know when you find it. It's kind of like falling in love. I might not be able to explain the process or how you get there, but you will surely know when you have found it.

My wife and I walked out of a Home Depot one day, saw a church sign across the parking lot, and said, "We should try that church next Sunday." We have now been there for years and it was our right one. We also walked into others that we immediately knew were not the right ones for us. So good luck with your quest.

CHAPTER 13
Some Final Thoughts...

I know that not everyone will agree with me, but look around at the world we find ourselves living in. Nearly 400 years ago, a group of men and women, called Pilgrims, risked their lives and traveled thousands of miles in tiny wooden ships to wild, untamed land in search of freedom. For them, freedom meant the ability to practice their religion, whatever it may have been. These early brave people would be the forerunners of those who would eventually create a nation we now know as the United States of America, a nation founded on godly principles, but not based on any single religion. These early men and women came to America, a safe place where they would be free to practice whatever religion they chose and where they could freely worship their God without government interference of any kind.

Somewhere along the way, this nation veered off course. We now have a nation where the open practice of religion is frowned upon and, in many cases, even forbidden. We can't speak of God in our schools or in most public assemblies lest we offend someone. We have been told so many times that our constitution forbids allowing us to speak of God in our public institutions. We have been taught a fallacy that the Constitution requires separation of church and state, a term that does not exist anywhere in the constitution. No matter how many times you may have heard it, it is still false! The first amendment to our constitution states, *__Congress shall make no law__ respecting an establishment of religion, or __pro-__*

hibiting the free exercise thereof. That's it, there is no other mention regarding religion. It clearly was meant to protect against the government establishing a 'state religion.' Congress shall not establish a religion, period. And Congress shall not prohibit or interfere with the free exercise of anyone's religion. We have to remember that the Constitution was intended to protect citizens from the government and its overreach and not the other way around. The courts have taken us a long way down a path of government interference and have so distorted not only the intentions of the framers but the specific language of the first amendment. There seems to be a fear that by allowing the freedoms protected by the Constitution, that somehow it might be viewed as showing favoritism to any one religion. The result is that instead of the freedom stated in the constitution, we now have limitations imposed on the rights that the document was clearly intended to protect.

I'm not going to go into how this distortion came about, but I ask you to simply look around; you will see the results of the denial of God in our lives and in our institutions. We have mass shootings happening on a far too frequent basis. I can't even count how many school shootings have occurred just during the time that I was writing this book. We see our children being murdered in their schools, people shot in movie theaters, malls, meaningless drive-by shootings, and shootings in our workplaces. We have more division in this country than possibly any time since the Civil War. We have more suicides than at any time in our history, and in Michigan alone, a person commits suicide every six hours—every six hours! Today we find there is no longer a place for political disagreement; we either agree with a viewpoint or we hate any person with a different view. We hate, we literally hate and want to do harm to those who dare to think differently than we do. Put a bumper sticker on your car for a political candidate and you just might get your car 'keyed;' put a political sign in your yard and you might get a brick through your window or worse, and folks, it isn't getting any better.

I am not saying that if we all 'get religion' that bad things will stop happening, our children will be safe in their schools, and no one will shoot up a church or a shopping mall ever again. Of course, bad things will happen. Jesus promised us that bad things will happen. What He promised us was that He will never leave us, and when we lean on Him, He will give us the strength to endure, and in the end, He will take us home to be with Him forever. God is not something we made up in our minds; He is real. God created us with a hole, a place within each of us created as a place for Him to reside. We have all tried to fill that hole with things other than Him and find that it just doesn't work. It is like trying to put a square peg in a round hole. That spot within us is a hole that only He can fill. It is the spot that when God takes up residence there, we experience peace and joy in our lives.

We live in an evil fallen world, but these mass murderers, these people committing suicide every day, are crying out. People who have truly trusted God have truly accepted His grace, are at peace within and they do not kill others or themselves. Sure, there are the mentally ill who may not be miraculously healed by having God in their lives any more than having God in our hearts does not necessarily protect us from cancer or any other disease.

But take a good look; this is what a godless society looks like, this is what a nation that will not allow us to speak of God in our schools, pray before a football game or dare to put a cross on 'public' land, looks like.

There are now, and there will probably always be, those who say that man created God out of a need for something or someone to lean on, a crutch. But the reality is that God created man out of His love, and He makes Himself available to lean on whenever we need Him. Do you think that maybe we are a nation, a world, in need of a God? You tell me!

Let me leave you with this one final thought. God is saying this to you: "I loved you so much that I created you so I could share my love with you. You turned your back on me, you sinned, yet I still loved you. I loved you so much that I sent my Son to become man, to suffer and die to pay the price for your sins. I paid your debt because I love you and want you to be with me forever." What are you waiting for?

"Waiting to come to the Lord when you get your life cleaned up is like waiting to go to the ER when you stop bleeding. He doesn't love some future version of you; He loves you in your mess."

References

1. 'Dann, C. (2019, August 25). 'A deep and boiling anger': NBC/WSJ poll finds a pessimistic America despite current economic satisfaction. Retrieved from https://www.nbcnews.com/politics/meet-the-press/deep-boiling-anger-nbc-wsj-poll-finds-pessimistic-america-despite-n1045916

2. Research from the course. (2019, February 19). Retrieved from https://talkingjesus.org/research-from-the-course/

3. Lawrence Mykytiuk, "Did Jesus Exist? Searching for Evidence Beyond the Bible" Biblical Archaeology Review, January/February 2015

4. The Annals of Imperial Rome, Cornelius Tacitus, Dorset Press, 1984

5. Angelo, M. (2018, June 5). The Opened Door: How Chuck Colson's Legacy of Hope Lives On. Retrieved from https://www.prisonfellowship.org/2018/04/chuck-colsons-legacy-hope-lives/

6. The Case for the Resurrection: A First-Century Investigative Reporter Probes History's Pivotal Event, Lee Strobel, Zondervan, 2009

7. What Would Jesus Do?, InTouch Ministries Daily Devotional, June 20, 2019, (n.d.). Retrieved from https://www.intouch.org/read/magazine/daily-devotions/what-would-jesus-do

8. Warren W. Wiersbe, Wiersbe's Expository Outlines on the New Testament, David C. Cook, 1992, James, page 721

9. Warren W. Wiersbe, Wiersbe's Expository Outlines on the New Testament, David C. Cook, 1992

10. Warren W. Wiersbe, Wiersbe's Expository Outlines on the Old Testament, David C. Cook, 1993

11. Murashko, A. (n.d.). EXCLUSIVE Rick Warren: 'Flat Out Wrong' That Muslims, Christians View God the Same. Retrieved from https://www.christianpost.com/news/exclusive-rick-warren-flat-out-wrong-that-muslims-christians-view-god-the-same-70767/

12. Lee Strobel, The Case For Christ, Zondervan, 1998

13. Rice Broocks, God's Not Dead: Evidence of God in an Age of Uncertainty, Thomas Nelson Publishers, 2013

14. Frank Turek, Stealing from God: Why Atheists Need God to Make Their Case, Navpress, 2015

15. James, M. A. (2018, February 1). Confidence in our Identity. Retrieved from https://servinggodenthusiastically.wordpress.com/2018/02/01/confidence-in-our-identity/

CPSIA information can be obtained
at www.ICGtesting.com
Printed in the USA
BVHW070636070320
574164BV00001B/47

9 781734 303230